· CONCISE GUIDE TO ·

# Arthritis in the Horse

## Also by David W. Ramey, D.V.M.

Horsefeathers: Facts Versus Myths About Your Horse's Health

Concise Guide to Medications and Supplements in the Horse

Concise Guide to Tendon and Ligament Injuries in the Horse

Concise Guide to Navicular Syndrome in the Horse

Concise Guide to Colic in the Horse

Concise Guide to Nutrition in the Horse

The Anatomy of an Horse

· CONCISE GUIDE TO ·

# Arthritis
# in the Horse

*David W. Ramey, D.V.M.*

Howell Book House
New York

Howell Book House
A Simon & Schuster Macmillan Company
1633 Broadway
New York, NY 10019-6785

Macmillan Publishing books may be purchased for business or sales promotional use. For information, please write: Special Markets Department, Macmillan Publishing USA, 1633 Broadway, New York, NY 10019-6785.

MACMILLAN is a registered trademark of Macmillan, Inc.

Library of Congress Cataloging-in-Publication Data

Ramey, David W.
    Concise guide to arthritis in the horse / David W. Ramey.
      p.   cm.
    Includes bibliographical references and index.
    ISBN 0-87605-091-7
    1. Horses—Diseases.   2. Arthritis in animals.  I. Title.
    SF959.A78R35  1998
    636.1'0896722  dc21                 97-52816
                                         CIP

Manufactured in the United States of America

10 9 8 7 6 5 4 3 2 1

# CONTENTS

# CONTENTS

# Acknowledgments

In 1982, when the author was a senior in veterinary school, a young professor, who had completed a Ph.D. in anatomy but had not yet made his mark, took the author into the pathology laboratory. There, the author was treated to the most comprehensive, understandable, unforgettable and engaging discussion of equine anatomy that he was to experience. The author went on to private equine practice and to write some books; the professor, Dr. C. Wayne McIlwraith, went on to become arguably the foremost expert in the study of joint disease in the horse. Now, as then, I am thankful to be able to follow his lead.

As with the previous books in the series, Lynda Fenneman provided the helpful illustrations. Special thanks are in order to Dr. Natalie Eddington of the Department of Pharmaceutical Sciences in the School of Pharmacy at the University of Maryland in Baltimore, who gave of her time to make sure that the information on oral joint supplements was accurate and timely. To help make sure that the book was understandable and readable, Karen Abbott, my wonderful secretary, gave wonderful advice. Linda Rarey, who, as it turns out, has horses in her blood (see John), provided her keen insights as well. Jonna Dennis added her thoughtful comments all the way from Texas. Finally, my wife, Elizabeth, who is responsible for many of the other good things in my life, found the time in her busy schedule to chip in with a few suggestions, too. Jackson, the new addition, can't read yet.

# INTRODUCTION

If you own a horse, one of the reasons that you might have for doing so is so that it can perform. Whether your horse is used for jumping, dressage, reining, pleasure, driving or any one of a myriad of other events, your horse is an athlete. For him to perform at his athletic best, all of his parts must be in good working order.

One reason why your horse might not be able to perform to its capabilities is because of lameness. When a horse is limping, it's because at least one of his many parts isn't working properly. Although there are many reasons a horse may go lame, injuries to and disease of the joints are among the most common ones. Perhaps, as much as anything else, this is merely a matter of probability; there are over 200 joints in the horse's body, so the chances that something might eventually go wrong in at least one of them are pretty good.

Without question, horse joints get a lot of attention. Evaluation and treatment of the joints of the horse take up a big part of the daily duties of an equine veterinarian. The care and maintenance of joints is a major concern for trainers, grooms and owners, as well. If it seems as if everyone is worrying about the joints of your horse, it's because they most likely are.

One of the things that frequently goes wrong in a joint is the process of arthritis. Simply stated, arthritis is inflammation of a joint. However, the process of arthritis is far from simple. In fact, it is a complex process that can involve any of the numerous structures that make up a joint.

Furthermore, arthritis is not a well-defined process that occurs in the same manner in every horse or in every joint. Veterinarians are commonly asked to treat what appear to be at least two distinctly different types of arthritis. "Acute" arthritis appears to be related to joint trauma and over-use and is seen commonly in racing horses, for example. Osteoarthritis (also called degenerative joint disease) is seen primarily (although not exclusively) in older horses and involves a complex series of events that ultimately results in the breakdown and destruction of the joint. Although the two types of arthritis are different in many ways, they are certainly related. Sometimes (but not always), acute arthritis can even lead to osteoarthritis.

Arthritis is an area of active and rapidly changing research. It is also a relatively new area for science to investigate. A great number of medical and surgical treatments exists for various conditions of horse joints. Many of the treatments used today have only appeared in the last ten years; the effects of other treatments that have been used for a longer period of time are just beginning to be understood. Many of these treatments have not been well evaluated as far as their true effectiveness; many times the treatment of choice varies according to the individual who is doing the treatment.

Acute arthritis can often be controlled with no resulting long-term damage to a joint; unfortunately, no cure currently exists for osteo-arthritis. Obviously, arthritis is also a problem in many species besides the horse. A cure for arthritis would be a tremendous boon to people, as well as horses. However, at this time, there is no one "proper" treatment of any type of arthritis in the horse (nor is there a "proper" treatment for any other species). Rather, there are many treatment options, all of which may have some merit depending on the situation.

This book is intended to help you understand your options. It will help you understand what a joint is and how it works. It will teach you what happens when normal joint function is impaired by joint disease. The book will explain the most commonly used treatments for arthritis (and some related joint problems) and help you understand the pluses and minuses of each. It will also help give you a realistic idea of what you can expect to happen to your horse as a result of his arthritis and the likelihood that it will be helped by treatment.

This book will also explore other types of joint problems that occasionally affect the horse and cause joint inflammation. The final chapter is devoted to two of these subjects: osteochondrosis (a complex disease of the joints of primarily young horses) and joint infections, which are a frequently devastating problem, especially if they are unrecognized or untreated. Both of the aforementioned conditions are associated with inflammation of a joint; thus they are included in this book.

It is appropriate to be concerned about your horse's joints. It is also appropriate to want to take care of any problems that occur in them in the best way possible. The information in this book should help you decide the most appropriate way to care for your horse and understand the many treatment choices that present themselves to you (and your veterinarian). Working together, you and those whom you enlist to help your horse will hopefully be able to come up with a plan for effective treatment of your horse's diseased joints. If the joint doesn't respond to treatment, perhaps this book will help you to understand why. There is some comfort to be gained by knowing that you've done all that you can do. At the very least, this book should help you satisfy that goal.

# CHAPTER I

# The Anatomy and Physiology of a Normal Joint

ON ITS SURFACE, A JOINT SEEMS LIKE A VERY SIMPLE structure. In fact, by definition, a joint *is* simple. Anywhere that bones meet in the horse's body is called a joint. A joint allows bones to bend.

However, this simple definition belies a very complex structure. The normal workings of a horse's joint involve the interaction of diverse and unique structures with functions and activities found nowhere else in the horse's body. It's essential to have a good understanding of what these structures are and what they do so that you can understand what happens when they become affected by disease.

## JOINT ANATOMY

### Bone

If you were to design a horse from scratch, you would face an interesting engineering dilemma. How would you support the great size and strength of the creature? You would have to come up with some sort of a scaffold for the body that was strong and stiff enough to support the loads imposed on it by the weight of the horse and the tremendous mechanical forces associated with movement. The scaffold would have to be made from some material that would not be appreciably damaged or deformed by the load of the horse, yet it still would have to be able to adapt to the stresses put upon it. The horse's (and every other mammal's) answer to this engineering dilemma is bone. Bone serves as a scaffold for the horse's body and as the place where many important tissues attach.

Bone is not a static tissue. It is alive; it is dynamic and ever-changing. An inborn genetic code determines the size and shape of a normal bone. Thus, the horse's body knows from conception what its pastern or cannon bone is eventually going to look like. However, in addition to the external size and shape changes that occur as the horse grows, bone can also change its internal structure. The bones of the horse, especially those of the lower limbs, are particularly sensitive to the stresses of physical activity. As a direct result of those stresses, bone can be removed from some areas and added to others. This sort of activity goes on throughout the life of the horse.

The bone in a joint supports all of the joint's tissues. Without healthy bone, a joint begins to collapse. In fact, disease of the supporting bone may well be a primary focus of disease in horses that develop arthritis. In some horses, the cumulative effect of the stress of physical activity on the supporting bone can overwhelm the ability of the bone to compensate for the damage that the stress causes. This can have devastating consequences for normal joint function, as you will see. The bone in and around a joint can become involved in a disease process called arthritis.

## Cartilage

Cartilage is a very complex and specialized tissue. It's critical for normal joint function. Because of its critical function in normal joints, many of the current therapies for arthritis are directed specifically at the cartilage. Two major types of cartilage are important in the study of joints.

Hyaline cartilage covers the ends of the bones where they meet to form a joint. Hyaline cartilage is also often referred to as articular cartilage (*articular* means "joint"; another name for a joint is an articulation). The articular cartilage provides a smooth gliding surface where the ends of the bones are in contact with each other. Amazingly (and importantly) this contact is almost frictionless. This means the two bones that meet in the joint can move against each other with a minimum of wear on the surfaces of the joint that are in contact with each other. (Exactly how it does that will be discussed later in this chapter.)

Articular cartilage is made up of about 70 percent water. Of the non-water part of cartilage, about half is made up of a protein called collagen. Collagen provides the framework that makes up the cartilage, much as bone makes up the framework that supports the horse's body. The collagen is concentrated near the surface of the cartilage; here it helps the cartilage resist the strain applied to it during weight bearing. Most of the rest of cartilage is made up of water and a complex group of proteins called proteoglycans.

Along with collagen, proteoglycans make up the structure of normal joint cartilage. These various chemical compounds appear to be critical in, among other things, helping the cartilage resist being squished as the horse bears weight on the leg. Among the most important proteoglycans are two that have been used in various therapeutic applications in the horse: hyaluronan (commonly referred to as hyaluronic acid) and chondroitin sulfate. These substances will be discussed at length in this book.

The joint cartilage is maintained by a group of cells known as chondrocytes. These cells actually make up only a fairly small percentage of the total volume of the cartilage, but they have an importance that belies their numbers. The cartilage cells maintain and replace the

3

cartilage tissue by synthesizing the proteoglycans, collagen and other components that make up the cartilage. Unfortunately, the cartilage cells appear to have a very limited ability to repair injured cartilage. This has tremendous implications when it comes to how the horse's body deals with cartilage that gets damaged through trauma or inflammation.

To try to visualize what articular cartilage structure is like, think of a big, stiff sponge. The sponge is made up of collagen fibers. In the spaces between the fibers of the sponge are the proteoglycans (which look like little bottle brushes from a chemical structure point of view), stiffly filling the spaces. Scatter some cells into the sponge and fill it all up with saltwater (all body fluids contain salts) and there you have it (Figure I)!

The second important cartilage of joints is *fibrocartilage*. Fibrocartilage has a different structure than does the cartilage covering the ends of the bones (its structure is not important for the purposes of this book). Fibrocartilage isn't normally found in very many joints. It mostly occurs in the stifle joint of the hind leg, where it forms two little cushions (each one is called a *meniscus*). These cushions sit between where the *femur* (the long bone that comes out of the hip) contacts the *tibia* (the long bone that runs down to the hock). The menisci have been shown to help add to the stability of the joint as well as to act as shock absorbers. Although a meniscus can tear and become involved in a joint injury (as is seen in human athletes), fortunately such problems don't appear to be all that common in the horse.

Fibrocartilage is also significant because of its role in the repair of injured joints. When a joint surface is injured, the horse's body attempts to repair the injury. Unfortunately for the joint, articular cartilage appears largely unable to repair its structure. Instead, it heals itself with fibrocartilage. This very different type of cartilage does not generally do an adequate job in repairing the injured joint surface(s). (There's more on injury to and healing of joint cartilage in the next chapter.)

## · Figure I ·

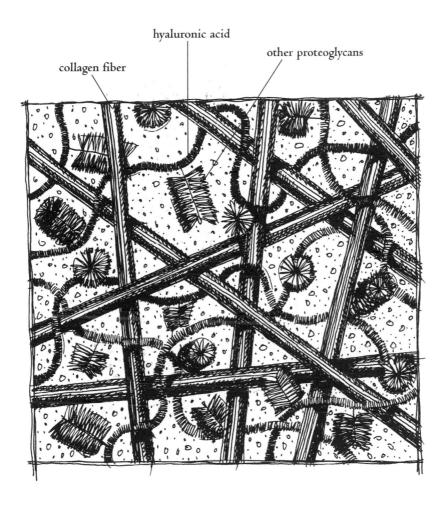

*Collagen fibers make up the framework of joint cartilage, like the fibers of a sponge. Scattered throughout are hyaluronic acid, chondroitin sulfate and other proteoglycans.*

## Joint Capsule *and* Synovial Membrane

The joint capsule is the wrapping paper around the package that is the joint. The outer portion of the capsule is a tough, thick, fibrous tissue that helps support and stabilize the joint. In it are also found the blood vessels and nerves for the joint. (The joint capsule also contains lymphatic vessels, which move tissue fluid, but these vessels do not appear to be especially important in the discussion of arthritis.)

Lining the joint capsule is the thin *synovial* membrane (the word "synovial" implies that the membrane is able to secrete a fluid). The synovial membrane has an importance that's out of proportion to its thinness, however. First, it produces the hyaluronan found in joint fluid, as well as other substances required for normal joint lubrication. Second, the joint fluid that is inside the joint is a result of filtration of the blood that occurs in the membrane (the blood vessels of the joint capsule go right up to the inner surface). Finally, the cells of the synovial membrane also have a function known as *phagocytosis*. This impressive word refers to the ability of a cell to eat up and remove things that shouldn't be in the body, such as bacteria or other foreign substances. The synovial membrane is a big deal (insofar as joints are concerned).

If the synovial membrane is injured, bad things can happen inside the joint. Unfortunately, because of its relative thinness and fragility, the synovial membrane often *is* injured. The response of the synovial membrane to injury and the effects of injury on the membrane are important contributors to the process of arthritis and other joint diseases in the horse.

## Joint Fluid

Inside each joint is a specialized synovial fluid, formed by the cells of the synovial membrane of the joint capsule. There are normally a few cells in the fluid, a little bit of protein and lots of hyaluronan (but it's from a different source from that which occurs in the joint cartilage).

Joints can't function properly without fluid in them. The fluid serves several specialized purposes, including:

1. Joint lubrication. The lubrication provided by the joint fluid is not merely like the lubrication provided by the oil for your car's engine. It's quite complex. (There's more on joint lubrication later in the chapter; understanding joint lubrication is critical to understanding what you're trying to do when you treat an arthritic joint.)

2. Cartilage nutrition. The joint fluid provides the nutrition to the cells that maintain the joint cartilage.

3. Removal of waste products. The process of metabolism (which is the process of life) produces metabolic waste products. The waste products formed by the metabolism of the cells of the joint cartilage are removed by the joint fluid.

Normal joint fluid is a clear, straw-yellow color. It's also kind of slimy and thick; when you let it drip from the end of a needle, it tends to hang together and string out (sort of like honey). This property is called the *viscosity* of the joint fluid. Although you'd think otherwise, the viscosity of the joint fluid is not at all important for its normal function. However, the viscosity of the fluid can change, particularly when the joint fluid is affected by the process of inflammation (other properties of the joint fluid can change with inflammation, too: more on that in the next chapter). Thus, examination of the joint fluid can become a very useful diagnostic tool in the evaluation of arthritic joints.

## Ligaments, Tendons and Muscles

Ligaments are straps of tissue that usually connect a bone to another bone. Tendons connect a muscle to a bone. Muscles connect bones to each other and move bones closer to each other when they contract. (Contraction, which is active, and relaxation, which is passive, are the only things that muscles can do.) These three structures are all important for joint stability.

Any of these three types of tissue can occur in (in the case of ligaments) or around (in the case of all three) joints. These are tough bits of tissue that serve to keep bones in stable position relative to each other. For example, in the shoulder, the various large muscle groups strap the shoulder joint in place like a harness; in the lower limb, the ligaments of the fetlock joint and the tendons that run over the top of them act much like the strapping tape that you would use to tape two boxes together prior to putting them in the mail. The joints of the upper part of the limbs are surrounded by more muscle and have few ligaments; the joints of the lower part of the limbs rely on such things as joint capsules, tendons, ligaments and even the fact that the joint surfaces are contoured (so they'll fit together like pieces in a puzzle) for their stability. There's no muscle in the lower limb of the horse to help stabilize the joints.

If ligaments, tendons or muscles that help stabilize joints become disrupted due to injury, instability of a joint can result. Normally, joints have a well-defined range of motion. The bones in the joint move in relation to each other as much as possible. However, that movement is restricted by one or more of these three structures. If, for example, a ligament on the side of a joint becomes disrupted due to injury, a range of motion that was not previously available to the joint can occur. (Using the example of the boxes taped together, say that you cut the tape on one side of the box. You could now open up a space between the boxes where the tape had been cut. The position of the boxes would no longer be firmly fixed. That's the sort of thing that occurs when ligament, tendon or muscle injury causes joint instability.)

Instability in a joint is a bad thing. Joint instability causes abnormal loading to be placed on joints. The bones in an unstable joint move in relation to each other in ways that they normally can't. This results (rather quickly, actually) in arthritis. Thus, an injury to a tendon, muscle or ligament can have severe secondary consequences in a joint. Injury to these structures needs to be recognized and treated quickly and properly (and there's a *Concise Guide to Tendon and Ligament Injuries in the Horse* to give you a hand with that).

Figure 2 puts the pieces of the joint puzzle in perspective.

# How Joints Work (Joint Physiology)

Every joint in the horse's body has a defined range of motion. That is, the bones that make up a joint can move in relation to each other only over a given range of movement. For example, the horse's fetlock joint can move over a range of 270 degrees, which is three-quarters of a circle. This range of motion is controlled by the muscles, which contract and relax. It is also limited by the tendons and ligaments that go around and (occasionally, in the case of ligaments) through the joints, by the joint capsule and by the shape of the bones themselves. This range of motion repeats itself with each movement of the horse. Thanks to the smooth articular cartilage and the lubricating action of the joint fluid, the movement of the ends of the bones against each other is almost without friction. Of course, this is very significant; if there were friction in a joint, it would cause the cartilage to wear out over time as the ends of the bones rubbed against each other.

The lubrication that occurs in a joint is much more complicated than the type of lubrication that occurs in a car's engine. In a car engine, a thin film of oil sits between the engine parts that rub together (the pistons in the cylinders of the engine) and thus helps to prevent friction. While this type of lubrication may occur in a joint (with the joint fluid being

· Figure 2 ·

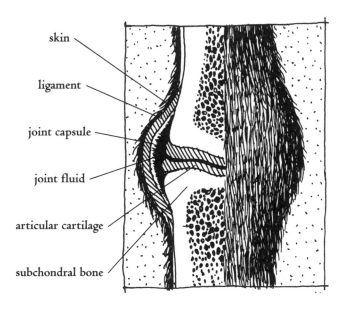

skin

ligament

joint capsule

joint fluid

articular cartilage

subchondral bone

*The normal anatomy of a horse's fetlock.*

the oil for the engine), at least six other types of lubrication may occur, too. The type of lubrication that predominates at a particular time in a joint is largely dependent on the type of stress that's being applied to the joint. For example, one type of lubrication, called *weeping* lubrication, occurs because the weight of the horse actually squeezes a layer of fluid out of the cartilage and into the space between the two joint surfaces, where it then acts like the oil in an engine. Weeping lubrication is thought to be especially important when the joint is moving at high speeds.

Another important type of lubrication is called *boundary* lubrication. Boundary lubrication is the function of hyaluronan (and another joint molecule called lubricin). Boundary lubrication helps the soft tissue of the joints move over the cartilage surfaces. It predominates between the inner lining of the joint capsule and the edges of the joint surfaces. Boundary lubrication is most important when the horse isn't moving at all or is moving at very low speeds.

The whole subject of lubrication in a joint is brought up mostly to illustrate that it's not as simple a concept as you might think. Thus, hyaluronan, a substance that's commonly injected into horse joints as a treatment for arthritis, should not be thought of as some sort of joint "oil," that is, merely as a way to help lubricate the joint. (There's a whole chapter on hyaluronan later in the book.)

In addition to providing a smooth gliding surface for the ends of the bones, cartilage also helps to absorb the stress that's placed on the ends of the bones by the tremendous body weight of the horse. It's a truly wondrous system that works in a number of ways.

The collagen fibers that make up the framework of the cartilage help to resist the tensile strain that occurs during weight bearing. Tensile strain is the tendency of a force to try to tear something apart. In the case of the horse's joint, the tensile strain comes from the force of the weight and movement of the horse's body. Collagen fibers are found in highest concentrations near the surface of the cartilage, where the tensile forces applied to the joint are presumably the highest.

The proteoglycans that are found between the collagen fibers occur in highest concentrations deep in the cartilage. Here, along with the water that's normally in the cartilage, it's felt that they help to resist the compressive strain that occurs when the horse bears weight on the limb. Compressive strain is the tendency of a force to try to squish something together. The effect of the proteoglycans and the water in the cartilage is similar to what would happen if you tried to push a board down into a pail of water, if the board were cut to perfectly fit the pail (so that the water in the pail couldn't splash out over the sides of the board). You might be able to push the board down into the water a little bit initially, but pretty quickly the water would stiffen and become impossible to compress further. Again, it's the weight of the horse that's the culprit in providing the compressive stress to the joint.

So what happens in a normal limb joint when a horse moves? First, the action of the muscles moves the bones, which move in relation to each other through a joint. The movement of the bones is controlled and restrained by the tendons, ligaments and the joint capsule. As the horse strides, the leg moves through the air and finally lands on the ground.

When the horse's leg hits the ground, the important joint functions of weight bearing and shock absorption begin. The weight of the horse on the joint causes the joint cartilage to mold and bend. The cartilage surfaces that touch each other tend to flatten, increasing the contact area between the two joint surfaces and cushioning the impact. In addition, as the joint surfaces are crunched into each other, they tend to become more stable and resist the compression caused by the horse's weight. The weight squeezes fluid out of the cartilage; this provides important joint lubrication, lubrication that is assisted by the action of hyaluronan and other molecules found in the joint fluid. Since the cartilage surfaces are smooth and well lubricated, there is very little friction between them as the bones contact each other and move. As the horse moves forward, the leg comes up off the ground, and the cycle is repeated.

## How Movement Affects Joints

What happens to the joint when the horse moves? The mechanical forces of movement and exercise are sort of a double-edged sword for a joint.

Without movement (when a horse's leg is completely immobilized in a cast, for example), all sorts of bad things begin to happen to a joint. The supporting tendons and ligaments get soft and lax. The joint capsule gets thicker. The joint cartilage begins to show signs of deterioration on radiographs (X-rays). The cartilage thins out and loses some of its proteoglycan content. Loss of supporting bone occurs. Anyone who has ever been in a cast can attest to the fact that some rehabilitation is required to restore the joints that were encased in the cast back to normal.

Thus, normal exercise and movement are not only helpful to maintain the health of a joint; they're also critical. In species other than horses, it's been shown that exercise strengthens the supporting tissues of a joint. It improves the proteoglycan content of the cartilage. It causes strengthening of the bone. Normal exercise may help pump the joint fluid in and out of the cartilage, helping to bring in the nutrients that the fluid provides the cartilage cells and helping to remove the waste products that they produce. Cartilage cells also respond to exercise by helping to maintain the cartilage. Under normal circumstances, movement of the horse's limb can occur over and over again with little damage or wear to the joint.

However, it is possible to get too much of a good thing. Too much exercise is clearly bad for a joint. Too much high-intensity exercise increases the risk of injury to tissues. It causes cartilage to get thicker and stiffer. In dogs, too much exercise causes the proteoglycan and hyaluronan levels in the cartilage to decrease. High-intensity running is also associated with breakdown of the cartilage surface. (All of these changes are seen in the process of arthritis.)

Too much stress on a joint appears to be able to overwhelm the ability of the cartilage to maintain itself. Unfortunately, to date, no studies have been done looking specifically at the response of horse joint cartilage to different types of training and exercise regimens. There may also be some variation between individuals in the amount of exercise that they can tolerate. Unfortunately, nobody knows exactly how much exercise is too much for a joint. Thus, at this point in time, proper training of horses is as much of an art as it is a science. Accordingly, too much high-intensity exercise appears to be one of the most important factors predisposing any horse to the development of arthritis in its joints.

# CHAPTER 2

# The Process of Arthritis: Inflammation and How It Affects Joints

WHEN JOINTS ARE NORMAL, HORSES ARE ABLE TO MOVE their bodies and limbs in a pain-free, normal manner. When joints are abnormal, horses cannot function at their peak performance level. The key to understanding why and how joints become abnormal is understanding a complex and fascinating process called inflammation.

The word "inflammation" comes to the English language from the Latin word for "to set on fire." It's an apt term, since inflamed joints are often sore and hot. The word "arthritis" means inflammation of a joint; the suffix "-itis" is used in medical terminology to indicate inflammation is occurring in a structure.

Inflammation is actually a protective mechanism initiated by the body in response to an injury. Although there are conditions where inflammation is a generalized response throughout the body, usually inflammation is localized to a particular area of the body (for example, a joint). The process of inflammation is set off by injury to or destruction of body tissue.

Inflammation can actually be a good thing; it is the initial response in a series of events that lead to the ultimate repair of the injured tissue. The purpose of inflammation is to destroy, dilute or isolate both the injured tissue and/or the foreign (to the body) agent that caused the injury (if there is one). Most joint problems in the horse are caused by some sort of injury to tissue and don't involve any foreign agents. However, if there is inflammation in a joint caused by some sort of a foreign agent such as a bacteria, for example, the horse's body sets off an aggressive inflammatory response that tries to isolate and remove the bacteria.

The signs of inflammation have been recognized for thousands of years (they were first described by Roman physicians). The classic signs of inflammation that are seen in a horse's joint (or in any inflamed structure) include heat, pain, swelling and loss of function. (Redness of the skin, which is a commonly described sign of inflammation in people, is not usually visible in horses because of their hair coat.) Therapy for inflamed, arthritic joints is directed at reversing the signs of inflammation—that is, at eliminating heat, pain and swelling and restoring normal joint function.

On a microscopic level, inflammation involves an intricate series of events that especially affect blood vessels in the inflamed area. Inflammation causes blood vessels to dilate; one effect of this dilation is to bring more blood into the inflamed area (that's why the end of your finger gets red when you hit it with a hammer and inflame it). Blood vessels are just little tubes formed by layers of cells. When blood vessels become inflamed, small gaps appear between the cells. Thus, another effect of inflammation on blood vessels is to allow fluid and cells to leak out of the little gaps and into the inflamed area.

The cells that are released into joints and joint tissues during inflammation are mostly white blood cells (that's really their color). White blood cells are the body's police force. They are enlisted by the horse's body to chew up and remove the injured joint tissue. They do so by releasing a variety of chemicals and enzymes into the inflamed area.

The enzymes and chemicals that are released into an inflamed area help break down and destroy injured tissue so that an attempt can be made at removing and replacing it. (Although the names of the chemicals aren't really important for the purposes of this book, you will hear terms like "free radicals" bandied about the barn from time to time when discussing arthritis therapy. Free radicals are just one of many types of potentially damaging substances that can be released into an inflamed joint.) Unfortunately, these chemicals and enzymes aren't at all specific in their effects. They can break down and destroy normal tissue, too. Thus, one of the goals of controlling the process of inflammation is to control the bad secondary effects of naturally occurring inflammatory chemicals and enzymes on normal structures.

Inflammatory fluid is different in composition from the fluid that's found in normal tissue. Since the inflammatory fluid comes from the blood plasma (plasma is the fluid part of the blood), it contains lots of protein. Typically, inflammatory fluid can be distinguished by, among other things, the higher level of protein in it than in normal fluids. If the inflammation is severe or unchecked, the inflammatory proteins tend to mature and form clots. This can result in the formation of fibrous bands that cause structures to abnormally stick together (these fibrous bands are called *adhesions*). If an injury is bad enough to destroy blood vessels instead of merely inflaming them, bleeding into the injured area occurs. The presence of blood in a joint is often an indication of a more severe joint injury or even a fracture of the bone in the joint.

The existence of protein-containing inflammatory fluid or blood in a joint can be useful in helping to determine the extent or severity of an injury. As inflammation subsides, the joint fluid returns to normal. This can be used to help monitor treatment progress.

# The Two Types of Inflammation

Inflammation is usually divided into two distinct types although both types can exist simultaneously in some unfortunate horses. The two types of inflammation can arise from many causes; what they all have in common is the underlying disease process. The principles of treatment and the likelihood that the arthritis problem can be resolved depend directly on the type of inflammation that's present.

## Acute Inflammation

*Acute* inflammation in a joint typically occurs suddenly from injury to or overuse of a joint. It's the sort of thing that happens to you when you suddenly sprain your ankle or do three back-to-back aerobic workouts (instead of the one that you are used to), for example. The process of acute inflammation is characterized by all of the classic signs of inflammation and all of the inflammatory changes that were just described. Acute inflammation is commonly seen in racing horses in the joints of the front legs, especially the fetlock and knee joints, or in jumping, dressage or reining horses in the joints of the hind legs, especially the hocks.

Acute inflammation isn't limited to sprains and overuse, however. Acute inflammation accompanies joints that are infected with bacteria (see chapter 9 for more on joint infections). The acute inflammation which occurs in joints that have been affected by a fracture of the supporting bone represents another unique situation (and there's more information on joint trauma later in this chapter). Still, although there are some differences in the various manifestations of acute inflammation, most of the underlying changes in an inflamed joint are present no matter what the particular situation.

## Chronic Inflammation

*Chronic* inflammation in a joint is slowly progressing and uncontrolled (and sometimes uncontrollable). Chronic inflammation can be the continuation of acute inflammation; however—and this is very important—*not all acute inflammation leads to chronic inflammation.* This means that just because your horse has an episode of acute arthritis, he won't necessarily develop a chronic, deteriorating joint as a result of it.

Importantly, chronic inflammation is characterized by the formation of new tissue. It usually causes permanent tissue damage in a joint. That damage is generally irreversible. This is the process that people think of when they refer to having a "bad" hip or knee. In horses, chronic inflammation of joints shows up in such colorfully described conditions as ringbone or bone spavin.

The process of uncontrolled chronic inflammation in a horse joint is referred to in the medical field as osteoarthritis or degenerative joint disease. In most cases, this group of joint problems is characterized by a progressive and permanent loss of the joint cartilage and changes in the bone, joint capsule and synovial membrane. It's the cartilage loss that's especially troublesome. Once it's gone, it doesn't come back.

Nobody is sure what starts the process of osteoarthritis or why some (but not all) joints that become acutely inflamed eventually develop the problem. However, for the purposes of understanding the problem, it may be useful to consider three separate categories of osteoarthritis:

1. As a problem that develops secondary to long-term inflammation of the joint capsule and synovial membrane.
2. As a result of and associated with other problems such as joint fractures or infections.
3. As an incidental finding in a joint that has responded to some sort of mechanical stress caused by the weight and movement

of the horse. Importantly, this type of osteoarthritis does *not* necessarily progress to worse things.

Osteoarthritis is the cause of tremendous losses in the horse industry in terms of decreased performance and lameness of horses affected with the condition. It is a cause of lost sales in horses that are even *suspected* to have the condition. Osteoarthritis is a frustrating condition for veterinarians to treat because it is, at least at this point in time, incurable. There is much more to come on this important subject.

# THE EFFECTS OF INFLAMMATION ON JOINT STRUCTURES

No one is exactly sure just where the process of inflammation begins in a joint and what the earliest changes are that lead to the development of arthritis. However, arthritis can cause changes in each of the structures that make up a joint. It's unlikely that any of the changes that are described occur independently of the other; in fact, all of the structures of a joint are interrelated. When one part of the ship begins to sink, the whole thing can eventually go down (if the hole's not patched first).

The trick to successful treatment of arthritis is to recognize and correct an acute problem before it becomes chronic. Unfortunately, this isn't always possible. For example, some joint fractures cause acute changes to the joint that will inevitably result in chronic arthritis, no matter what you do. Chronic arthritis, when it occurs, is such a difficult problem at least in part because, with the exception of the bone, none of the joint tissues that become involved in chronic arthritis can ever return to their normal function. Thus, to understand arthritis, it's a good thing to look at the changes that occur in each structure to help you understand what's going on in an inflamed joint.

## Joint Capsule and Synovial Membrane

Inflammation of the joint capsule is called capsulitis. If the joint capsule becomes inflamed, it becomes thickened, swollen and very painful. Try bending a horse's leg that has a sore joint capsule, and your horse might try to pull his leg out of your hand (or worse) for your trouble. If inflammation of the joint capsule persists, it can become permanently thickened. This can result in a reduced range of motion for the joint (try bending your finger when it's swollen, inflamed and sore).

You can most easily appreciate a reduced range of motion in the ankle joint of a horse who has had episodes of capsulitis. Normally, this joint is very flexible and easy to bend. In a horse who has had repeated episodes of inflammation of the fetlock joint, the joint can become very stiff and inflexible.

Inflammation of the synovial membrane that lines the joint capsule is known as *synovitis*. The response to inflammation of the synovial membrane is much like that of the joint capsule, although since the synovial membrane is much thinner than the joint capsule, it's hard to say how much it contributes to the mechanical problem of joint stiffness. It's probably a moot point; inflammation of the synovial membrane is most likely always accompanied by joint capsule inflammation as well.

However, due to the fact that the synovial membrane is such an important structure, inflammation of it can have some profound consequences for the joint. In fact, synovitis may initiate some of the very first changes to occur in the process of arthritis. It almost certainly plays a part in all types of arthritis.

When the synovial membrane is inflamed, chemicals associated with the process of inflammation are released into the joint. These chemicals (which have rather long and arcane names like interleukin and stromelysin) go to work on the joint cartilage. They have the same effect on joint cartilage that acid has on a metal etching plate. In addition, inflammation of the synovial membrane stimulates the nerve fibers of the joint. While this undoubtedly causes some of the pain associated with an inflamed joint, the nerve fibers themselves may release substances into the joint that damage the joint cartilage.

Inflammation of the synovial membrane can have other bad effects as well. An inflamed synovial membrane doesn't work normally. This can cause the joint fluid to back up. It may also result in an increased production of joint fluid. Either way, more fluid increases pressure in the joint, which in turn increases pressure in the underlying bone. Increased bone pressure is another reason that arthritis may be painful for the horse.

After repeated trauma or injury to the synovial membrane, the synovial tissue can even become permanently changed. It may get replaced by fibrous scar tissue and the reddish granulation tissue that's associated with wounds in the horse. This synovial membrane replacement tissue never restores the original function of the original membrane. In addition, this abnormal tissue is associated with the joint stiffness, increased pain and decreased production of joint fluid that can be seen in joints that are chronically inflamed.

## Bone

Arthritis may begin as a disease of the bone that underlies the cartilage. The disease process may sometimes start as a result of bone failure from the chronic wear and tear that's put on a joint by exercise. Exercise-induced stress to the bone can cause microscopic fractures. This sort of fatigue failure is the same sort of thing that you see when you bend a paper clip back and forth until it snaps. You really don't appreciate all the changes that are going on inside the metal of the paper clip as you bend it back and forth until it's too late (and the paper clip snaps).

As bone is injured from the inflammation caused by joint wear and tear, it changes. The bone initially responds to the stress by getting harder (the medical term is called *sclerosis*). While this may serve to help reinforce the bone, it may also decrease the shock absorption that goes on underneath the joint cartilage and result in a lack of support for the cartilage—it's as if the cartilage were sleeping on the floor instead of a mattress. Both decreased shock-absorbing capacity and destruction of the underlying bone result in damage to the overlying cartilage. This is the physiologic equivalent of kicking the legs out from under a table. You kick out the legs (the bone under the cartilage), and the tabletop (the cartilage) comes crashing down!

Additional new bone can also be produced in a joint as a direct result of inflammation. Bone responds to inflammation by producing more bone. (That's at least one of the reasons why when you break your arm, the bone is able to heal itself.) However, in and around a joint, the production of more bone is not necessarily a good thing. New production around a joint is commonly referred to as bone "spurs." However, not all bone spurs mean the same thing for a joint, nor do they all have the same cause. There are two distinct situations in which more bone is commonly produced as a response to inflammation.

The first occurs at the point where the joint capsule or a ligament that surrounds the joint attaches to the bone. If either of these structures becomes inflamed (as they frequently do), the inflammation can also cause more bone to be produced in the areas of the attachments. Remember, once it gets going, inflammation never limits itself to a particular tissue. The attachment of a joint capsule, tendon or ligament onto a bone surface is called an *enthesis;* the spurs that result from inflammation at the attachments are called *enthesiophytes. Importantly, the existence of enthesiophytes around a joint does not necessarily mean that the joint affected by them is going to develop osteoarthritis.* In fact, normal joints can have "bone spurs" in them with no signs of arthritis. The spurs are presumably some sort of adaptive response by the bone to help reinforce areas of stress in the joint capsule or ligament attachments.

However, bone spurs are not always benign. They can also be a sign of underlying arthritis in a joint. New bone and bone spurs can be produced in a joint affected with osteoarthritis. These spurs are properly called osteophytes (*osteo-* means bone). As the cartilage in an arthritic joint becomes destroyed over time, the underlying bone is revealed. That newly revealed bone then becomes inflamed and begins to produce more bone. This is a terrible thing for a joint. Instead of the smooth, gliding cartilage surfaces that exist in a normal joint for the bones on either side of the joint to move against, the surfaces of an osteoarthritic joint are inflamed, hard bony surfaces that are poorly suited for normal joint function.

The production of new bone and bone spurs in and around an osteoarthritic joint is sometimes so characteristic that it has been given descriptive names in some instances. For example, osteoarthritis of the horse's pastern can cause a "ring" of new bone and bone spurs to be produced around the joint. This condition has been recognized in horses for a long time; the term *ringbone* is hundreds of years old (Figure 3).

Obviously, it's important to be able to tell the difference between bone spurs that are no big deal and those that are a big problem for the horse. The interpretation of X-rays is one of the jobs of your veterinarian. There's more information on X-rays of joints in the following chapter.

## Joint Fluid

The inflammatory chemicals released by the synovial membrane into the joint fluid break down the fluid and change its character and composition. This fact can be used to assist in the diagnosis of joint disease.

In addition, with acute joint inflammation, more joint fluid is produced than normal (some of you have undoubtedly experienced this phenomenon if you've twisted your knee). Extra fluid in a joint causes

· Figure 3 ·

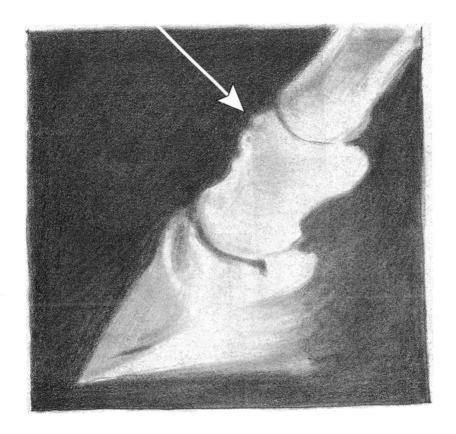

*Arthritis of the pastern (ringbone) causes new bone (arrow) produced in and around the joint. This X-ray shows "high" ringbone; "low" ringbone occurs in the joint of the foot.*

pain. Extra fluid stretches the tissues of the joint capsule and synovial membrane, stimulating the nerve fibers there. The extra fluid also raises the pressure inside the joint; this may get in the way of the flow of blood in the synovial membrane and thereby reduce the amount of vital oxygen available to the joint (which is associated with its own set of problems).

## Cartilage

Ultimately, all of the inflammation that occurs in and around a joint affects the articular cartilage. Furthermore, the likelihood that the horse will ultimately recover from his arthritis directly depends on what happens to the cartilage. If the cartilage is relatively undamaged by an injury and/or inflammation, the joint will usually be fine. However, if there's enough cartilage damage to the joint and osteoarthritis and new bone formation begins to develop, the joint will never regain its normal function.

Unfortunately for a joint, articular cartilage appears to have a very limited ability to heal itself. When it does try to heal, it does so using tissue that's not normal for the joint surfaces such as fibrocartilage. In addition, the other tissues of the joint that *can* repair themselves, such as the synovial membrane, often try to get involved in the process of cartilage repair (the body is always trying to do anything it can to heal itself). Unfortunately, when the other tissues get involved in cartilage healing, they produce tissues that have different properties from normal joint cartilage. These tissues don't perform the functions of cartilage nearly as well as cartilage does.

Whether a cartilage injury can heal itself appears to be influenced by several things. First is the depth of the injury. The deeper a cartilage injury goes into the cartilage (the closer to the underlying bone it gets), the less likely that the injury is going to be able to repair itself. Second is the size of the injury. Larger injuries to cartilage are less likely to heal than are smaller ones. Horses can lose a good deal of cartilage and still be all right, however. In fact, horses with a loss of up to 30 percent of their joint cartilage have made a successful return to racing even though their cartilage has not healed. Third is the location of the cartilage injury. Certain spots on the joint surfaces bear more weight than others; if a cartilage injury occurs in a weight-bearing area, it will be less likely to heal. Fourth and finally, the age of the horse with a cartilage injury is important in the chance that the injury will heal. Foals and young horses apparently have some capacity to heal cartilage that is lost as the animal gets older.

Obviously, cartilage trauma can be caused by a sudden, severe injury. Cartilage can go from normal to abnormal very quickly if a horse steps in a hole and breaks a bone. Although this type of an injury can have some devastating consequences for a horse, it's not at all difficult to understand how it happens and why the cartilage gets hurt as a result. Fortunately, this sort of thing happens rather infrequently. Current techniques in fracture repair, which are touched on in chapter six, can save many of these horses. (No, you don't necessarily have to shoot a horse who breaks his leg.)

Of much more interest to those who study the process of arthritis is what are the earliest changes that happen in the cartilage as a result of joint inflammation. Unfortunately, the first changes that occur in diseased cartilage are not exactly clear. These processes are generally not apparent until the disease has progressed to where it's too late to reverse the changes. For example, racing horses that fracture little chips of bone off the front of their knees or fetlock joints frequently do so from areas in which it can be shown that there was already pre-existing damage. Horses that are diagnosed with osteoarthritic conditions such as ringbone or bone spavin are presented because they are limping; it can be determined that the affected joint has osteoarthritis, but by the time the diagnosis is made, it's too late to reverse any of the changes in the joint that have already occurred. It would be of great use if veterinarians (and medical doctors) could detect early changes in joints that could be stopped before more severe damage or injury resulted.

So what are the earliest changes that occur in diseased joints and cartilage? They appear to be several. You've already been introduced to the changes that occur in the bone under the cartilage. The stiffness of the underlying bone that results from inflammation may cause the cartilage to suffer increased wear and tear as a result of abnormal shock absorption in the joint. In addition, severe exercise stress, such as racing, may put abnormal stresses on the joint cartilage. It's thought that stiff bone or abnormal exercise stress may begin to break down the collagen of the cartilage, causing the physical structure of the cartilage to begin to disintegrate (remember the paper-clip example). As you remove collagen cards, eventually the whole house will weaken and collapse.

Another very early change that occurs in diseased joint cartilage is the loss of proteoglycans and changes in their structure. As these important chemicals are lost, the water content of the cartilage increases. Cartilage with increased water content becomes softer and is less able to withstand the forces that are placed on it. Diseased cartilage is more likely to be injured than is normal cartilage.

It's not at all clear which is the earliest change in an arthritic joint, collagen breakdown or loss of proteoglycans. However, it is clear that when you combine these two processes with the harsh chemicals that are released during the inflammatory process, the cartilage can be in for a lot of trouble. Furthermore, since cartilage has no nervous supply, damage to the cartilage can occur without causing pain for the horse. Trying to discover the trouble before it's too late is one of the great challenges facing modern medicine.

## Ligaments, Tendons and Muscle

Inflammation of ligaments, tendons and muscles can directly affect joints by destabilizing them.

Experimentally, arthritis can be created in a joint by cutting ligaments; clinically, arthritis is seen in joints that have had ligament injuries. Apparently, when you cut a joint ligament, the joint moves beyond its normal range of motion. This causes the joint surfaces to wear abnormally and ultimately causes them to break down. Inflammation of ligaments, tendons and muscles, when it occurs, also adds to the pain of arthritis.

# THE CAUSES OF ARTHRITIS IN HORSE JOINTS

Everyone wants to know why things happen (even if it's just so they'll have someone to blame). In the case of medicine, to the extent that you can find out why things happen, you might be able to keep them from happening again. Thus, there's a lot of medical research directed at finding out why joints become arthritic.

To a certain extent, changes in joints are caused by the "stuff happens" theory of medicine. That is, it's part of the overall scheme of life. A horse is asked to run; a joint gets overstressed; an inflamed joint results. Such injuries are the risk that any athlete takes. Even if a horse does not compete at high levels, inevitable alterations in the joints occur. For example, as horses (and all animals) age, changes occur in the proteoglycan content of cartilage. Contrary to popular belief, arthritis is *not* an inevitable consequence of aging. Although these joint changes are not the same as those seen in arthritis, they do occur; they are certainly not beneficial and no one knows why they occur. Stuff happens.

However, one of two underlying causes generally sets off the events that lead to arthritis (and both causes may occur at the same time). If the resultant arthritis cannot be controlled (or is uncontrollable), new bone formation and osteoarthritis will be the result.

The initiating insult that results in new bone formation in a joint may be mechanical. That is, the insult may occur as a result of the stresses applied to the joint by the horse's body weight and movement. These stresses may be an accumulation of normal forces (like the breaking-the-paper-clip example) or they may be the direct result of some abnormal force. An abnormal force might occur as a single incident (say, when a horse steps in a hole). Abnormal forces might accumulate in a joint due to poor limb conformation, where the joints are loaded in an abnormal fashion over time because of the way that the horse is put together. Alternatively, abnormal forces on a joint may occur acutely from fatigue of the muscles, tendons and ligaments that normally help support the joint. If these structures tire, a joint may exceed its normal range of motion. Tissue injury may be the end result.

Day-to-day wear and tear from moving around and exercising is thought to be the number one culprit in starting the whole process of arthritis. Clearly, some exercise is beneficial for joints. However, repeated or excessive trauma to a joint may begin to wear down the various tissues in the ways described earlier and/or cause the joint to become inflamed. Such trauma may be no more than excessive exercise; for example, in young horses, elevated levels of weight bearing tends to cause changes in the cartilage that are normally only seen in older or aging horses.

Low-motion joints, such as the lower joints of the hock or the joints of the pastern, seem to be particularly susceptible to wear-and-tear injuries. These joints don't move very much under normal circumstances. Low-motion joints such as the pastern or the lower joints of the hock are particularly susceptible to stress-induced changes in the joint caused by mechanical forces; since these joints don't move much, the mechanical stress placed on them literally tries to tear them apart (Figure 4). Horses that use their hind ends a lot, such as cutters, jumpers, reiners and dressage horses, develop problems in the hock and pastern joints quite commonly, especially as they age and the effects of the stress accumulate.

Chemical injury can also set off the process of arthritis. Chemical injury commonly results from any of a number of causes of joint capsule inflammation and the resultant release of inflammatory chemicals. Chemical inflammation can also occur as a result of the presence of infectious bacteria in a joint or from the effects of drugs injected into joints.

Realistically, it's often impossible to separate the causes of arthritis. Mechanical injuries cause chemical changes to occur in the joint. Chemical injuries cause changes in the joint tissues that affect the mechanics of how the affected limb functions. These complex interrelationships add to the difficulties of trying to precisely determine (and describe) the causes of arthritis in joints.

# JOINT FRACTURES

Joint fractures are a unique form of acute arthritis in the horse. All of the changes that are seen with any type of acute joint inflammation occur in joints as a result of fracture. However, the treatment of joint fractures also entails some special problems, so it's worth taking a closer look at what happens to joints when enough trauma occurs in them to break bone.

The most common type of joint fracture that you'll see is the "chip" fracture that often occurs in the knees and ankles of racing horses (Figure 5). These fractures typically happen along the edges of the affected joints. It's thought that these injuries take place when the horse's

· Figure 4 ·

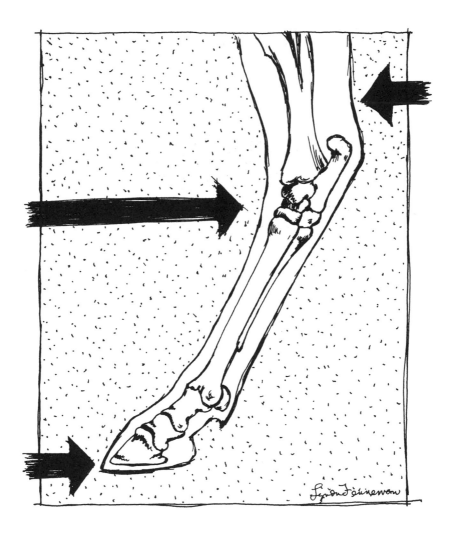

*While this horse is traveling to the left (upper arrow), when the foot lands on the ground (bottom arrow), it puts the brakes on the forward motion of the limb. These opposing forces concentrate at the hock (middle arrow).*

· Figure 5 ·

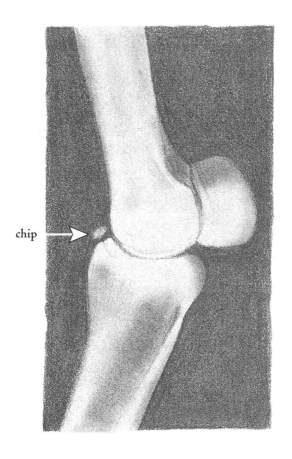

chip

*Chip fractures such as this one commonly occur in the fetlock joint of racing horses (arrow).*

leg bends too much (overextends). When the joint bends too much (say, at the end of a race, when the muscles, tendons and ligaments are tired), the bones move beyond their normal range of motion. Thus, the bones of the horse's knee, which are shaped like little building blocks and thus have well-defined edges, or the long bone of the pastern, which has a prominent lip on it, can bang into the bone that's above it and knock off a bit of the edge or the lip, respectively. These little bits of tissue are chunks of bone and cartilage.

While this sort of thing can occasionally be the result of a single episode of overextending, microscopic examination of joints with chip fractures has shown that the chips most commonly occur from spots where chronic wear and tear have taken place in the joint. That is, the underlying bone and cartilage from where the chip occurred can be shown to be diseased. Most of the time, when the chip breaks off the end of the bone, it breaks off from an area where unrecognized arthritic changes were already going on in the affected joint.

The most devastating types of joint fracture are the partial or complete failures that occur in the supporting bone. Like chip fractures, major fractures through a joint can occur through areas of diseased and damaged bone or cartilage. However, many times these disastrous injuries are an unpredictable result of a single episode of trauma.

Assuming that the fracture can be repaired (and not all of them can), the limiting factor in returning the horse with a joint fracture to normal is usually the cartilage. Bone can heal; cartilage cannot. The more cartilage that is involved in the injury, the less likely that the joint will ultimately ever be normal. Small chunks of bone and cartilage can be removed from a horse with no resultant problems and no development of secondary osteoarthritis in the future. Some small bone chips may not even need removal, particularly if the horse is intended to be used for pleasure or other types of non-racing events. (Contrary to popular belief, the chips don't float around in the joint; they are grabbed by the synovial membrane and held in one spot. Sometimes such chips are picked up on prepurchase examinations, where they cause a bit of consternation. They often don't seem to bother the horse at all, but they sure can worry the purchaser who's concerned about arthritis developing in the joint.)

However, if the smooth cartilage surfaces of a normal joint are disrupted as a result of the damage that's sustained by the cartilage in a joint fracture, normal gliding of the adjacent bones over each other can no longer occur. This sets the stage for chronic inflammation. In this case, osteoarthritis will eventually develop (although the more precise the repair, the more closely that the damaged cartilage is realigned by the repair, the less likely it is that arthritic problems will develop). Sometimes the fracture failure of a joint is so complete that the only way to salvage the horse's life is to destroy the joint entirely and fuse it. (There's more on joint surgeries in chapter six.)

You've just been presented with a lot of information on how and why joint injuries occur. It's a lot to digest. So here's a little review of some important facts for you:

- Understanding the process of inflammation is the key to understanding arthritis.
- Inflammation may be acute (sudden) or it may be chronic (long-term).
- Acute inflammation may or may not lead to chronic inflammation.
- Inflammation can cause changes in all of the tissues that make up a joint.
- The signs of joint inflammation reflect the changes that occur in the joint tissues.
- No one understands exactly the sequence of events that leads to arthritis.

- The underlying causes of arthritis are two: mechanical and chemical.
- Once cartilage is damaged, it can't heal.
- Arthritis is not something that you want your horse to have, but it may be unavoidable.

Having looked at how joints are affected by inflammation, the next step in dealing with arthritis is to understand how it can be determined that a particular joint is affected by it. Read on!

# CHAPTER 3

# The Diagnosis of Joint Disease

Veterinarians who work with horses spend a good deal of their time trying to figure out what makes a particular horse limp. The diagnosis of lameness related to arthritis is really no different from the diagnosis of any other type of lameness; arthritis is just one of many reasons a horse may limp. However, there are certain basic steps that are followed in obtaining a diagnosis of lameness in a horse. In the case of arthritis, many of these steps involve recognizing the classic signs of inflammation that were mentioned in the preceding chapter. In addition, several diagnostic aids are commonly used by veterinarians to help confirm their clinical impressions.

One of the biggest problems with arthritis is that some horses who have it *don't* limp. This is a particular problem with the earliest stages of osteoarthritis. Damage can be going on in a joint for a long time before the horse finally starts showing you that his leg hurts. In this way, arthritis is no different from any number of other medical conditions (like heart disease or lung cancer, for example) where you don't realize that something bad is happening until relatively late in the disease process. By the time the problem is recognized, it may be too late to do much about it. Thus, in the future, it's hoped that medical personnel will be able to recognize that arthritis is going on before bad and irreversible changes in the affected joint occur. In fact, trying to determine the earliest changes associated with arthritis in hopes of treating problems before they become irreversible is one of the most active areas of arthritis-related research. Unfortunately, medicine isn't there just yet.

# THE CLASSIC SIGNS OF INFLAMMATION AND HOW THEY RELATE TO ARTHRITIS

## Pain

The fact that your horse is suffering from arthritis-related pain is often quite evident. Pain may cause the horse to demonstrate obvious signs of lameness such as bobbing his head when he trots. (If the lameness is in the front leg, the head often goes up when the lame leg hits the ground and down when the good leg hits the ground.) Or there may be some obvious soreness to manipulation of the affected joint. If you actively bend a horse's sore joint, he'll most likely let you know that it hurts by trying to pull the leg away from you (or bite you or rear up in the air or demonstrate some other form of delightful behavior that indicates that he's not happy with you).

## Swelling

Swelling of a joint is seen in both acute and chronic arthritis. Swelling in and around an acutely inflamed joint occurs due to blood vessel dilation and the resultant movement of fluid into the injured tissue. This type of swelling is usually soft and sore to the touch. It may also cause the joint to appear larger than normal. Swelling in and around a chronically inflamed joint frequently feels hard due to the production of new bone that results from the long-term inflammatory process.

You can often see the area that's swollen, unless the joint that's affected is up high in the leg, such as the shoulder or hip. As has been noted before, many of the swellings are so typical that they've even been given names. For example, *bog spavin* refers to swelling of the tibiotarsal joint in the area commonly called the hock in the horse's back leg; *bone spavin* refers to osteoarthritis of the lower joints of the hock. (The term *spavin* apparently comes from an Old French word meaning "to hop around like a sparrow"; it may have been used to describe the gait of some horses affected with the condition.) You've already been introduced to the term *ringbone;* another term, *osselets* (from the Latin word for "little bones") is a racetrack term that usually describes swelling and soreness around the fetlock joints.

Most of these terms used to describe swelling in and around joints are literally hundreds of years old. However, although the terms are colorful, they really don't have any medical significance. From the standpoint of understanding what's going on in a horse's joint, terms such as osteoarthritis or acute inflammation are much more descriptive; nevertheless, the old horseman's terms are a lot more fun!

## Heat

It's been demonstrated that the temperature of acutely inflamed areas rises, often by as much as one degree above the normal body temperature. This can occasionally be of some diagnostic significance, particularly if a device that measures the local area temperature can be used (this diagnostic technique is called thermography). However, most people really aren't sensitive enough to detect a one-degree rise in the temperature of an area, particularly if it's hot outside. Chronically inflamed areas rarely have an increase in the local temperature. Thus, the presence of increased heat in an area, while an interesting finding when it can be de-tected, is generally not a particularly consistent or useful diagnostic tool.

## Loss of Function

Obviously, a sore, hot, and/or swollen joint doesn't work as well as a normal joint. This is best shown by manipulating the affected joint, which may be stiff, swollen, hot or painful, or by trotting the horse, who may be lame.

# DIAGNOSTIC STEPS THAT CONFIRM A CLINICAL DIAGNOSIS OF ARTHRITIS

Most of the steps that are taken to reach a diagnosis of arthritis in a horse's limb aren't any different from the steps used to reach the diagnosis of any other condition that causes lameness in a horse. Still, it's useful to review the steps used in the evaluation of a lame horse that particularly pertain to arthritis so that you'll have a good understanding of the process if it's going to be applied to your horse.

## Visual Exam

Since arthritic joints tend to be somewhat larger than normal joints due to swelling, you can often see them before you even touch the horse. If you suspect a problem, make sure that you look at your horse from a distance before you get too close to him to really see him. (Not being able to see the forest for the trees is a problem for some people.)

## Palpation

Palpation is a fancy word meaning "feeling." (You pay a lot of money to learn words such as these in medical schools.) It really doesn't take a lot of time to become fairly familiar with the relatively simple joint anatomy of the horse's lower limbs (Figure 6). Within a short time, you can determine which lumps are normal and which ones shouldn't be there. You also have the leg on the opposite side of the horse from the one that you are feeling to serve as a comparison; if a lump is on one leg but not the other, chances are it shouldn't be there at all. (Of course, if a lump is on both legs, it's either normal or your horse may have a couple of problems.)

In addition to feeling for various enlargements, the horse's limb can be manipulated to check for the soreness and decreased range of motion that frequently accompanies arthritis. For example, you should be able to fold a horse's knee so that the back of upper and lower limb touch; if you can't touch the limbs together or if the horse objects to your trying to do so, it's reasonable to suspect that the knee joint might be something of a problem for the horse. Similarly, horses with problems in the hock or stifle joints of the hind limbs frequently resent having their hind legs picked up or bent.

Before trying to check out a lame horse, you should familiarize yourself with the normal range of motion for the various joints of the limbs. If you then attempt to examine your horse, knowing the way that the normal horse feels, you'll be more likely to correctly decide if your horse actually has a problem or not.

## Flexion Tests

If you've been around horses enough, you've probably seen a flexion test. These deceptively simple tests are used to apply pressure to various structures (including joints) of the front or back leg. To perform a flexion test, you hold up the leg for a period of time, release the leg and trot the horse immediately off. Front legs are commonly flexed for about sixty seconds; for some reason, most descriptions of hind leg flexion tests

41

· Figure 6 ·

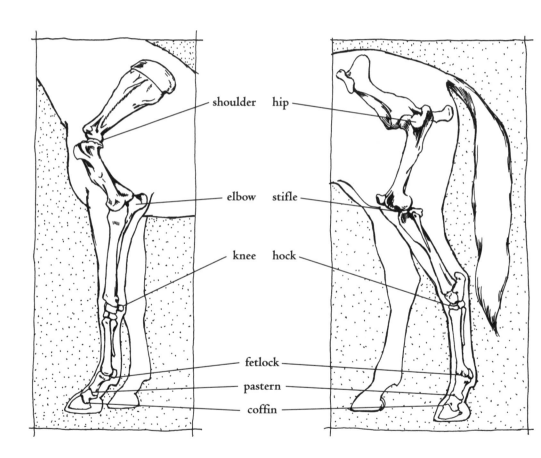

shoulder   hip

elbow   stifle

knee   hock

fetlock

pastern

coffin

*The major joints of the horse's fore and hind limbs.*

usually recommend ninety seconds. If the horse demonstrates lameness after his leg is released, this is a positive response to a flexion test.

Unfortunately, it's becoming apparent that flexion tests, especially those of the forelimb, are something of a can of worms. Research shows that although many normal horses with sore joints will demonstrate a positive response to a flexion test, so will horses with soreness related to other, non-joint structures. In fact, literally every single structure of the horse's forelimb from the carpus (knee) to the ground has been described as having a positive response to limb flexion if that structure has been injured. Furthermore, the response to the forelimb flexion test can also vary depending on how long you hold the limb in flexion, how hard you flex the limb and the age of the horse.

There hasn't been nearly as much work done examining the response of horses to hind limb flexion tests as there has been with forelimb flexion tests. Still, it should be fairly obvious that hind limb flexion tests aren't very specific either. Due to the way that his hind leg is put together, a horse cannot bend his hock without bending his stifle, fetlock and hip; if any of these joints are affected with arthritis (or any other problem), it would be expected that they would show a positive response to limb flexion.

In spite of their lack of specificity, flexion tests can be useful in reaching a diagnosis of joint problems such as arthritis. However, they have to be interpreted along with all of the other data gathered at the time of examination in order to come up with any reasonable conclusions. Remember this if you are buying a horse; just because a horse doesn't trot off sound after his limb is flexed, it doesn't necessarily mean there is a problem with that leg. In and of themselves, limb flexion tests appear to be of limited value.

## Anesthetic "Blocks"

One of the more common techniques used to assist in the diagnosis of lameness is the anesthetic nerve "block." The principle behind this technique is deceptively simple. If the horse has arthritis (or any other leg problem), the leg hurts. If the leg hurts, the horse limps. If, through the use of local anesthetic, you can make the spot that hurts go numb, the horse will stop limping. Then, by using this process of elimination, you'll have a good idea of the area from which your horse's lameness problem originates.

Joint disease is particularly amenable to diagnosis in this fashion. As you know, a joint is something of a self-contained compartment. Stuff that is put in the joint stays there (at least for a short period of time). Thus, if you put anesthetic directly into a joint and give it some time to slosh around—research has shown that it takes about five minutes—you can do a pretty effective job of numbing the joint and only the joint in most cases. A notable exception to this is the anesthetic block of the coffin joint of the foot; it's been well demonstrated that coffin joint block also numbs the navicular bone and some related ligaments. Other types of nerve blocks, in which the anesthetic is placed over nerves, localize soreness to generalized areas of the limb and are far less specific than blocks placed directly in the joint. If, after anesthetic is placed into a joint that is sore, the horse stops limping or at least shows a marked improvement in the way he travels, you can be pretty sure that joint is the source of the horse's lameness problem.

# DIAGNOSTIC STEPS THAT HELP DETERMINE HOW BAD THE JOINT PROBLEM ACTUALLY IS

Once you've determined that a horse has a problem with a joint (by whatever method), the next step in obtaining a diagnosis is to find out how bad the problem is. With this information, you can formulate a reasonable plan for treatment. You can also get a pretty good idea of the likelihood that the horse is going to respond favorably to the treatment that you select.

# Radiographs (X-rays)

Without a doubt, X-rays are the most commonly used tool in determining how bad a horse's joint problem really is. On the plus side, many X-ray machines are quite portable and lend themselves to use in the field. The X-rays themselves can be interpreted fairly easily and quickly (once you've been to school and seen enough of them). X-rays are of tremendous help in determining the presence of things like chips or chunks of bone and cartilage in a joint. They are also useful in assessing the growth of new bone in and around a joint or narrowing of the "space" between the bones in a joint that can be seen in association with various osteoarthritic conditions. (There really isn't a space between the bones of a joint. Since cartilage is mostly water, it doesn't show up on X-rays. If the cartilage is destroyed, the bones look closer together on X-rays.)

The minus side of X-rays is that they are not very sensitive, particularly since cartilage is invisible to them. There can be a lot of damage going on inside a joint with no corresponding changes on an X-ray of the affected joint. An X-ray abnormality may be just the tip of the iceberg; surgeons who do arthroscopy see this sort of thing all the time.

The other problem with X-rays is that it can sometimes be hard to determine if an X-ray "change" really means anything or not. It's well recognized that there is quite a bit of variation among X-rays of the joints of normal horses. That is, there may be some change on an X-ray of a normal horse that, while not common, is also not a problem.

This confusing situation is roughly analogous to people's feet. Most people stand with their toes pointing pretty much straight forward

However, some people are pigeon-toed; others stand with their toes pointing out to the sides. Which situation is normal? They all are for those individuals; the fact that one is more common than the other two doesn't mean that any of the three is abnormal. They are all variations of normal. In a similar fashion, the various lumps and bumps that can be seen on X-rays of normal horse joints can sometimes be just a variation of normal.

It's very important and sometimes very difficult to try to distinguish between the variations from normal that can occur in sound horses and the minor abnormalities that can be associated with the early stages of arthritis. In the case of normal variations, you don't want or need to be treating a horse for a problem when one doesn't exist. Similarly, you don't need to reject a horse that you are thinking about buying if the X-rays that you have elected to take are just a variation of normal, even if that variation is not particularly common. On the other hand, if X-ray abnormalities in a joint are associated with clinical lameness or such signs as stiffness or pain to joint manipulation, even minor changes can take on some great importance. Differentiating between the two situations is the job of your veterinarian. There are even veterinary radiologists (most of whom work at veterinary schools) who are happy to consult with you or your veterinarian and render an expert opinion to help you clear up a confusing X-ray dilemma.

## Arthrography

An arthrogram is an X-ray of a joint that's taken after you've shot some opaque (to an X-ray) liquid contrast material inside the joint. The contrast material fills up the joint space and outlines the structures inside the joint. Using this technique, the examiner can see the outlines of the joint cartilage, joint capsule, synovial membrane and menisci (if they are present). When it's applicable, arthrography is a nice technique because it's pretty easy to do although it's a bit more difficult to interpret. However, as other, better imaging techniques are developed, it's likely that they will replace arthrograms in the future; with the newer techniques you'll be able to get more and more accurate information without having to stick needles into the affected joint.

## Ultrasound

Ultrasound involves sending a sound wave into tissue and measuring the echo that's reflected back. It's a remarkable technology that's mostly used to look at the soft (non-bone) tissues of the body. However, in the right hands, it can also be a very sensitive method of looking in and around joints.

Ultrasound is pretty terrific for examining the tendons and ligaments around a joint. In certain cases it can even be used to examine the ligaments inside a joint such as the little cruciate ligaments that cross inside the stifle joint of the hind limb. It's a nice technology because one can see what's going on as the exam is done (unlike X-ray films, there's nothing to develop with an ultrasound machine), and the examiner can make any necessary adjustments or examinations from different angles while he or she is doing the exam. It can even occasionally be used to examine the surfaces of the joint cartilage. Ultrasound can sometimes pick up thickened areas of cartilage or irregularities in the joint surfaces that might be invisible to an X-ray. Ultrasound can be a much more sensitive imaging technique than X-ray in certain situations.

Unfortunately, due to their shape and/or location, some entire joints and parts of others are difficult or impossible to image with ultrasound. It can be pretty hard to look at structures deep within a big joint like the stifle. Ultrasound can't look around the curves that occur on many joint surfaces, either; this can sometimes make looking at the entire joint surface impossible. Of course, none of these things is really a disadvantage of ultrasound; they just reflect the current limitations of a technology for looking at joints that's still evolving.

## Scintigraphy (Bone Scan)

Scintigraphy—or bone scanning, as it is called in the interests of easy pronunciation—takes advantage of the fact that when a joint is inflamed and/or new bone is being produced, the blood vessels in the area are dilated. As you know, this means that fluid can leak out of the inflamed blood vessels. To perform a bone scan, a radioactive dye is injected into the horse's bloodstream (this poses no danger to the horse). The dye then comes out of the blood vessels and concentrates in areas of inflammation. The radioactive dye can then be detected with a special camera.

Scintigraphy is a pretty sensitive indicator of inflammation. It can show that an area is inflamed before changes are seen on X-ray or ultrasound. It can also pick up changes that can be missed on some X-rays, such as hairline fractures (fractures where the fractured bone hasn't separated enough to be seen). It can also be used to help decide if changes that are seen on X-rays are significant or not; if a change seen on an X-ray is not also shown to be inflamed on a bone scan, it's less likely that the X-ray change means anything bad is going on in the joint. It's also a nice technique because many different areas of the horse can be examined during the same exam. This is especially helpful if the horse has multiple areas of lameness.

Unfortunately, while very sensitive, scintigraphy isn't very specific. That is, it will show you where a problem might be, but it's unlikely to show you exactly what the problem is. Still, when used in combination with the various other diagnostic techniques, it's a very useful and well-accepted method to help uncover a horse's joint problem.

## Joint Fluid Analysis

The fluid that is within the joint can be a useful indicator of problems there. As you recall, normal joint fluid is a clear, pale yellow in color, and it's kind of thick. When things go wrong in the joint, all that changes.

Changes in the color of joint fluid are one signal that there may be a problem in the joint. If there are streaks of blood in the fluid, it may only mean that the needle your veterinarian poked into the joint caused a little bleeding. However, if the fluid is uniformly red, it suggests that there has been trauma to and bleeding into the joint. Dark-yellow or amber joint fluid can be an indication of previous bleeding into the joint; dark joint fluid is also a feature of joints that are affected with osteoarthritis. Joint fluid may lose its clarity due to bleeding or due to the presence of infection, with its accompanying inflammatory white blood cells and bacteria.

The consistency of the joint fluid can change with arthritis. When a joint becomes inflamed, the inflammatory products that are released into a joint cause some of the joint chemicals such as hyaluronan to break down. This causes the fluid to become thin and watery. Fortunately for the joint, the thinner joint fluid does not cause the fluid to lose its lubricating function. (Curiously, for some reason, some joints, especially the lower joints of the hock, seem to always have fluid that is thinner than that found in other joints.)

Acute inflammation and/or infection of a joint often cause an increase in the amount of joint fluid. This can often be seen as a bulging of the skin surfaces over the joint. When your veterinarian sticks a needle into a joint with increased fluid, sometimes the increased pressure will cause the fluid to shoot out in a stream!

Quite the opposite situation may be occasionally observed in chronically inflamed joints. Chronic inflammation can cause scarring and thickening (the medical term is *fibrosis*) of the joint capsule. This may result in a decreased production of joint fluid. Occasionally, when such a joint is tapped with a needle, it may not be possible to get any fluid out at all. However, just because fluid doesn't come out of a joint when it's stuck with a needle doesn't necessarily mean that there's a problem in there; sometimes the fluid just doesn't want to come out.

The composition of the joint fluid may also change when the joint becomes inflamed. For example, inflammation and/or infection will cause a measurable increase in the amount of protein that's in the fluid. White blood cells, the body's first-line defenders, which normally aren't found in joints, will begin to show up in the fluid when it becomes inflamed and/or infected. When there's an infection in a joint, bacteria may be present (although they may be hard to find).

While looking at the joint fluid can offer an excellent means of evaluating the degree of inflammation within a joint, unfortunately it can't tell you much about what's going on with the cartilage within a joint. It was once hoped that joint fluid particle analysis could help identify the degree of cartilage injury. As you go deeper into the cartilage, the cartilage cells change their shape; it was once hoped that the presence of certain cells or cartilage particles in the joint fluid could be correlated with cartilage damage down to the level where those cells were present. Unfortunately, false positives and negatives are a problem that has rendered this approach to diagnosis of joint problems less useful than it originally appeared that it would be.

## Arthroscopy

Arguably the most important advance in the diagnosis and treatment of joint disease in the horse (as well as in people) has been arthroscopy. Before the advent of this technique, if a joint was to be directly examined, the whole joint had to be opened up with a long incision. This resulted in all sorts of complications related to the healing of the various tissues that were injured by cutting on them. Arthroscopy changed everything.

An arthroscope is a rigid tube that uses fiber-optic technology and allows the operator to look inside the joint. Instead of a big incision, a little hole is made in the skin and joint capsule to let the tube in. When compared to opening up a joint with an incision, arthroscopy offers the operator a very close and clear look at a joint with relatively little trauma to the limb. It's really remarkable.

Most people think of arthroscopy as just a surgical technique to fix problems within a joint. While it is certainly that, it is also a very useful diagnostic technique. Because you look directly at the joint with arthroscopy, it's a much more accurate and specific method of diagnosing joint disease than the other (indirect) methods of examining joints that have been previously mentioned. Using arthroscopy, the examiner can see all sorts of things that elude other methods of diagnosis, including changes in the joint cartilage, ligaments that run inside some of the joints and problems with the joint capsule and synovial membrane. Of course, the big disadvantage of the technique is that it requires the horse to be completely anesthetized to perform it, so it's not something that you're going to have done in the field. However, this disadvantage is generally offset by the fact that the examiner will usually go ahead and try to help fix whatever problem is identified as long as he or she is in the joint anyway.

## FUTURE DIRECTIONS IN THE DIAGNOSIS OF ARTHRITIS

There are other ways of looking at joints that are commonly used in the evaluation of human joints which so far have not been used widely in horses. Example of these technologies would be CAT scans (CAT stands for computerized axial tomography; the technology involves taking a whole bunch of X-rays and having a computer put together a three-dimensional image) or MRI (MRI stands for magnetic resonance imaging; this technology involves magnetic fields passing through tissue with a computer again putting together an image). There seem to be two primary reasons for this failure to adapt available technology in the human field to horses.

First is the expense. Advanced medical technology is really expensive. You have to look at a whole lot of horses and charge a whole lot of money to pay for machines that cost a million dollars or more.

Second is the size and nature of the horse. If you've ever had an MRI, for example, the technology requires you to lie in a big tube for forty-five minutes or so. This requirement presents some rather obvious problems in its applications to the standing horse. (You could anesthetize the horse, but you can't have metal anesthetic machines around the tremendous magnetic fields that are generated by the MRI machine.) Still, even given the size and expense limitations, these existing technologies are being developed for the routine evaluation of arthritic joints.

Eventually, it's hoped that the earliest stages of arthritis can be diagnosed by a blood test. Researchers are trying to figure out ways to determine that increased bone and cartilage activity is going on in the horse's body before any changes in the joint can be seen. For example, exercise-induced trauma affects cartilage metabolism; a blood test that could detect the metabolic activity of the cartilage might be useful as an early indicator of joint disease or as a way to follow the effectiveness of agents chosen for joint therapy. If changes to the cartilage can be detected before they can be seen, it might be possible to prevent some cases of osteoarthritis that might otherwise develop.

# CHAPTER 4

# Physical Therapies for Joint Disease

PHYSICAL THERAPY FOR ARTHRITIC JOINTS IS AN IMPOR-
tant and often overlooked avenue of therapy for arthritic horse joints.
Perhaps that's because physical therapy is generally relatively inexpensive,
and you can often perform it yourself. Physical therapies are fairly easy to
understand and apply. They are generally performed with a specific ob-
jective in mind. Best of all, well-directed physical therapies really do seem
to help.

## BANDAGING

Bandaging a limb is an effective means of controlling swelling. Swelling
commonly occurs in injured limbs as a result of acute inflammation; the
blood vessels affected by inflammation let extra fluid, protein and cells
into the joint and surrounding tissues. Since there isn't room for all that
stuff in normal tissue, the tissue swells. Swelling itself can cause further
damage to injured tissue by stretching it. Also, swollen tissue hurts!

Applying pressure to an acutely swollen limb helps counteract the movement of fluid from out of the inflamed blood vessels. Thus, pressure from a bandage can help prevent tissue damage and control the pain of an injured joint. A bandage also helps to immobilize an injured joint; by doing so, it helps to prevent further tissue damage.

For the treatment of chronic arthritis, the benefits of a bandage are somewhat less obvious. Bandages won't help decrease the bad things that occur in joints affected with osteoarthritis. About the only benefit to be gained by bandaging a limb affected with chronic arthritis is the increase in temperature that occurs in the area under a bandage. However, some horses with joint stiffness due to chronic arthritis may benefit from keeping their joints warm under a bandage.

# Heat

The application of heat to a joint is a time-honored way to help relieve the joint stiffness that occurs in chronic arthritis. Heat applied to an area causes local blood vessels to dilate; in people, this effect seems to help sore joints move more easily. (Whether the same effect is seen in horses is anyone's guess.)

Heat is probably not the best thing to apply to an acutely inflamed joint, however. A therapy that dilates blood vessels applied to an area in which dilated blood vessels are part of the problem would certainly have the potential to make things worse.

# Cold

Cold therapy is one of the classic first-line treatments for acute inflammation. Cold causes blood vessels to constrict; the leaks that open up in inflamed blood vessels can be at least partially shut down for a short period of time when cold is applied to them. Thus, cold therapy on an acutely inflamed joint helps to control the swelling and pain that occur with acute inflammation.

Cold therapy can be applied to an inflamed joint in a number of creative manners: with a hose, with a chemical cold pack, with any number of fancy boots and devices or by just using ice. It should be left on the leg for only about thirty minutes as you can cause cold injury to tissue if you overdo it. However, since acute inflammation doesn't last very long, the application of cold to a limb doesn't need to go on for very long, either: a couple of days, at most.

# REST

With acute injuries to any tissue, rest is an important part of any therapy. You have to allow injured tissue to heal; continuing to exercise on tissue that is already hurt usually just makes the problem worse.

There are a lot of considerations when it comes to resting a horse with a joint injury. Depending on the severity and the type of injury, the length of the prescribed rest and the type of rest that is prescribed (stall, paddock or pasture, for example) may vary. For example, with many joint injuries, sixty days is kind of a minimum rest period; it takes at least that long, and often longer, for the joint capsule and any associated ligaments or tendons to heal. Sometimes the kind of rest that can be offered depends on the facilities available to the horse owner. Sometimes, even if rest is prescribed, the prescription isn't followed due to unwillingness of the owner, trainer and especially the horse to comply.

It's rare that an acutely inflamed joint has to be completely immobilized in a cast to be rested unless there's been a major fracture. In fact, complete immobilization of a joint should most likely be avoided when possible. Stopping movement in a joint for a period of more than a month results in loss of bone and cartilage due to wasting away of the tissue (the medical term for this phenomenon is *atrophy*; if you've ever had your arm or leg in a cast, you understand it very well).

Unfortunately, horses are pretty rotten patients when it comes to resting. Thus, rest for an injured horse needs to be monitored and controlled. The easiest and most common way that this is done is by leaving the horse in the stall. Stall rest is easy on the owner and surprisingly well tolerated by the horse. The biggest problem with stall rest is that horse owners fret that their horse will become a bucking lunatic if left in the stall. This just isn't very common. Just because you might go nuts if you were left in a 12-by-12 stall doesn't mean that your horse might, too. In fact, if you cut down on the feed you're giving your horse so that he doesn't get fat and overly energetic, pay attention to him and make sure that he has other horses to see, you will almost never see any problems with a horse tolerating stall rest. You also shouldn't be overly concerned about your horse losing muscle tone while being rested in the stall; horses have a good bit of muscular work to do in just supporting their own weight, and such muscle tone as is lost during stall rest returns very quickly once the horse is back to work.

You have to be careful with other types of rest. Even in paddocks, horses can overdo it pretty quickly. If a horse is intended to be rested in a paddock, it shouldn't be a very large paddock, or the injury won't be rested. In pastures, horses can run around whenever they want to (although they usually stand around a lot). Any joint injury that is intended to be treated by pasture "rest" had better be pretty thoroughly healed before the horse is turned out.

For most cases of osteoarthritis, prolonged rest isn't really called for. Sometimes horses are rested for a couple of days after injections of medications into their sore joints, but since osteoarthritic joints don't get better, you can't cure them by resting them. Although joint soreness may be reduced by resting a horse with osteoarthritis, the soreness often returns once exercise resumes.

# EXERCISE

It has been well-demonstrated that some exercise is necessary for normal joint health. Mild exercise appears essential to help maintain normal proteoglycan concentrations in the joint cartilage. Given that the goal of treating any horse with arthritis is to return it to exercise, the question is, "When and how do you do it?" As you might expect, the answer to the question is, "It depends." As with rest, the amount of exercise prescribed for an injured joint depends on the type and severity of the injury.

After joint surgeries, if possible, some passive exercise to the injured joint may be helpful. If a joint has been operated on, bending it fifteen to twenty times a day and continuing for thirty days after surgery may help to reduce post-operative stiffness and soreness. (Obviously, you can't do this after a surgery in which the joint is placed in a cast.) Passive exercise may help to spread around the nutrients provided in the joint fluid and may help reduce scar tissue in the joint that has had surgery. Be careful when you first try this, of course; if the horse's joint hurts after surgery, he's not going to appreciate your efforts to manipulate it.

Once you begin to allow the horse to move around, controlled exercise is called for. One of the more common ways to begin controlled exercise is walking the horse by hand. For some gentle, loving horses, hand-walking is a wonderful way for you to enjoy a stroll, knowing that you are helping to take care of your injured friend. However, for other, less understanding beasts, hand-walking is five to ten minutes of bucking, rearing, kicking and spinning that's guaranteed to fray even the steadiest of nerves. This sort of hand-walking experience (sometimes also called "barn skiing") isn't good for either one of you. Thus, it may be advisable to sedate some horses prior to taking them out for a walk. Alternatively, it may be easier to walk the horse by riding him instead of walking him by hand if you are able to control him better under saddle. Your weight most likely won't be a significant factor insofar as the arthritic joint is concerned. Whatever method of walking you choose to employ, as the injured joint heals you can increase the amount of walking.

Other types of controlled exercise include treadmills, swimming pools, lunge lines and hills. There's not really much data on the true benefits of these sorts of therapies. They all seem to have their pluses and minuses. For example:

1. Swimming pools allow for an early return to exercise with minimal stress on the arthritic joint. While that may be good for the heart and lungs, it's not necessarily good for the joints, since weight-bearing is required for joint health.

2. Treadmills allow for exercise to be fairly precisely controlled and allow the skeleton to bear weight; you can easily increase the level of exercise by tilting the treadmill or by adding the weight of a saddle and rider. However, treadmills are pretty expensive and require some maintenance. Also, not everyone has (or wants) one.

3. Horses returning to full use can be initially exercised on a lunge line. However, when lungeing a horse, you have to be mindful of the fact that lungeing tends to load more stress on the legs that are on the inside of the circle. Plus, some horses are so happy to be on a lunge line that they buck, kick and play with reckless abandon; obviously, this is exactly the sort of thing that you want to avoid when rehabilitating an injured joint.

4. Exercising a horse up a hill increases the intensity of exercise. When compared with training on a flat surface, exercise up a hill requires less time and can be done at slower speeds to get the same effect.

The last thing that you want to allow the horse with an injured or arthritic joint to do is to run around indiscriminately. Turning a horse out to run isn't necessarily kind. A horse who is taken from the stall to the arena and allowed to run free usually explodes the moment he is released. The stress caused by the sudden change from rest to explosive bursts of energy is extreme and requires completely healthy tissue to tolerate it. One of the most disheartening things that can happen is to watch your healing horse reinjure his leg while he's running around like a maniac.

Exercise helps relieve the pain, stiffness and soreness of an osteoarthritic joint. Most people have seen horses start out stiff and improve after a few minutes of exercise. The "proper" way to exercise horses with osteoarthritis of one or more joints is pretty much a matter of trial and error. You want to provide enough exercise to help relieve the problems and soreness without providing so much exercise as to cause more lameness. The level of exercise for a horse with osteoarthritis has to be determined for each horse.

You can often provide or direct the initial physical therapies for your horse. Medical therapies for arthritis should always be chosen and applied under the direction of your veterinarian. Still, you will undoubtedly want to participate in the selection of medical treatments for your horse's arthritic problem. The information that you need to help understand your choices is provided in the next chapter.

# CHAPTER 5

# Medical Therapies for Joint Disease

As a point of fact, there are only two types of arthritic problems: those you can cure and those that you can't cure. Acute arthritis is frequently curable; that is, you can make the problem go away, it won't necessarily come back, and it doesn't necessarily lead to problems for the affected joint down the road. Chronic osteoarthritis, on the other hand, is incurable. No matter what you do, no matter how much money you spend and how many products or therapies you try, once changes have taken place within the joint, there's nothing that you can do (at least at this point in time) to get things back to normal. Thus, when you are treating acute arthritis, you're trying to aggressively and permanently fix the problem. However, when you are treating chronic arthritis, you're generally trying to find ways to help make the horse more comfortable and to hopefully help slow down the insidious progression of the deteriorating joint.

Adding to the confusion of the discussion of medical treatments for arthritis is that there is no "right" way to treat every case. There is no single treatment for every arthritic condition that will work in every horse. Furthermore, there is no one best way that the available treatments can be used. Thus, the treatment that your horse will receive is generally based on the experiences of the person doing the treating. There are many treatment options from which your veterinarian can choose, all of which may offer some advantage to your horse. The pages that follow will give you much information that you can use to help understand and select possible avenues of medical treatment for your horse's joint problem.

# LINIMENTS, BLISTERS, SWEATS AND POULTICES

Liniments are liquid preparations, usually made with an oily base, that are applied to the skin. They are usually either rubbed into the skin or applied under a bandage. As a general rule, liniments cause the skin to be irritated. When the skin is irritated by the chemicals in the liniment (liniments usually contain such things as alcohol, iodine and menthol, among many other things), blood vessels on the skin surface dilate. In people, this brings a feeling of warmth to the area and helps to relieve joint stiffness and soreness. Of course, whether this same thing happens in horses is anyone's guess. If nothing else, the effort in applying a liniment makes the owner feel good. It may also be that some of the chemicals that are found in some liniments (for example, capsacin, which is the substance that makes hot peppers hot) block nerve transmission to sore areas. This would make the areas less sore but certainly do nothing to promote healing.

Blisters are caustic chemicals that are applied to a horse's leg. They cause tremendous inflammation and swelling of the skin on which they are applied. This is usually done in a misguided effort to "bring circulation" into an area to "promote" healing. Blistering is occasionally prescribed for horses with osteoarthritis but is used much more commonly in the treatment of tendon and ligament injuries. Research has demonstrated that blistering does not promote circulation to deeper tissues and merely inflames the skin. However, blistering does have one positive effect. Since horses get so sore and swollen after being "treated" by blistering, it is an effective—though somewhat barbaric—way to make sure that a horse rests his leg. Hopefully, this form of therapy will eventually take its rightful place along with bleeding and leeches in the annals of medical history.

"Sweating" a leg refers to a method of applying medications such as nitrofurazone ointment, DMSO, corticosteroids or glycerine to a horse's limb. The medication is usually covered with plastic wrap, then bandaged. The lack of air circulation around the leg and the fact that the bandage keeps heat from dissipating cause the limb to build up heat and to sweat. Sweat bandages (also called sweat wraps) do seem to be able to help reduce minor accumulations of fluid that occur in or under the skin. However, they do not appear to be particularly effective in treating injuries that occur in deeper structures, such as joints, since sweat wraps can't "drive" the medication that is placed on the skin surface into the deeper tissues as is commonly believed.

Poultices are moist substances made up of clay or other earthen materials that have been mixed with a variety of other medications. They are commonly applied to horse legs in an effort to help reduce limb swelling. As the poultice agents dry, they may tend to have some local dehydrating effect on the skin surface and may make the skin feel tighter.

As applied to humans, poultices are generally warm, moist mixtures of things such as hot water and linseed meal. As such, poultices may help provide some heat to the tissue on which they are applied. In horses, however, most commercially available poultice preparations are kept in a bucket at room temperature. It's not at all obvious why such things would have a beneficial effect when placed on an arthritic joint.

# DMSO (Dimethyl Sulfoxide)

DMSO is a chemical solvent that has been credited with more than thirty properties for the treatment of disease. It is used in a wide variety of applications in the horse, including for the treatment of arthritis. DMSO comes in a liquid or a gel form; the liquid is frequently mixed with other medications. The liquid form can be used on top of the skin, orally and even intravenously (it has to be diluted to be given IV); a study was done in which it was even injected directly into a joint, with no apparent ill (or beneficial) effect. The gel form is always used on top of the skin.

DMSO is primarily an anti-inflammatory agent. It works in many different ways, the most important of which seem to relate to its ability to neutralize some of the destructive chemicals that are produced during the process of inflammation. Amazingly, as frequently as it is used, there are no standard dosages that have been generated for DMSO and no controlled studies that have been done to evaluate its effectiveness as a treatment for arthritis in horses; fortunately, DMSO is a very safe substance. The use of DMSO is usually based on the experiences of the person who's prescribing it.

DMSO is unique in that it can go through the skin without hurting it. It can also be used as a carrier of other substances through the skin. This has some potential benefits; for example, when DMSO is mixed with corticosteroids, the level of corticosteroids in the tissue has been shown to increase by three times.

DMSO is very volatile. It is rapidly absorbed into the bloodstream when it is applied on the skin. When the DMSO gets to the lungs, however, it comes out of the blood and is breathed out. Thus, DMSO can end up on the tongue after it is put on the skin. People who get DMSO on their skin frequently report an unpleasant taste of garlic or onions (or worse). Although this isn't at all harmful or dangerous, it certainly is not the sort of thing that you want to be applying to your horse before you have a nice meal.

## MSM (Methylsulfonyl Methane)

MSM is a substance that has been promoted as a treatment for arthritis (and many other conditions that cause lameness) in the horse. It's chemical structure is similar to that of DMSO. Proponents of MSM say that when it is fed to the horse, MSM acts like a "dietary" DMSO in that it can rummage around the horse's body and help remove by-products of inflammation.

Unfortunately, there's absolutely no scientific evidence that MSM does what is claimed. In fact, the only thing that can be stated with any certainty about MSM is that it is a source of dietary sulfur for the horse; that's no big deal because there's no known requirement for sulfur in the horse's diet. MSM certainly doesn't appear to be able to hurt the horse; it's just that if you are expecting a lot from MSM in helping to relieve your horse's arthritis, you may well be disappointed.

## Corticosteroids

Corticosteroids are potent agents in the fight against inflammation. In the treatment of joint disease, they are most commonly injected directly into the affected joint. There, they appear to have a terrific ability to help minimize the inflammation that occurs in both acute and chronic arthritis. Even though the drugs don't have any direct pain-relieving effect, if you can make the inflammation in a joint go away, the pain follows.

The first reported use of corticosteroids in joints occurred in 1955. Among other things, that means there hasn't been a lot of time to investigate such things as the differences between various corticosteroid drugs, the proper doses of the various drugs and all of their effects and side effects. This sort of work has really just begun over the past several years.

Unfortunately, prior to recent investigations of the effects of the drugs, much of the discussion about the use of corticosteroids in joints centered on whether they are good or bad. Most of this talk apparently stemmed from a report in 1968 that said corticosteroid injections into the joints of horses caused the joints (and the horses) to rapidly break down. Unfortunately, this report has been widely repeated. As a result, many horse owners and veterinarians alike have approached the use of corticosteroids in joints as something of a double-edged sword, being beneficial in the relief of joint inflammation on the one hand but having the potential to destroy the horse on the other. This same sort of thought has plagued human medicine regarding the use of corticosteroids. The tenacity of this idea is remarkable, given that literally millions of steroid injections are given into joints every year and that there are almost no reports of resultant joint destruction in the medical literature!

Work that is emerging suggests that not only do the fears of tremendous damage from therapeutic use of corticosteroids in joints appear unwarranted, but the drugs also have some wonderful beneficial effects in inflamed joints. They appear to be able to help stop inflammatory cells from moving into inflamed joints; they help fight the swelling by decreasing the tendency of the local blood vessels to leak fluid; and they inhibit production of chemicals associated with pain and inflammation. They are able to suppress the enzymes that can begin to destroy the joint cartilage when they are released into inflamed joints. In fact, some studies have shown that corticosteroid injections into joints actually *protect* the cartilage and may even have constructive effects on joint health. (For example, therapeutic doses of triamcinolone have been shown to increase proteoglycan synthesis in the joint.)

Granted, no drug is all good. Corticosteroids do have their problems. Their presence in a joint increases the potential for joint infection. Although the drugs are placed in the joints, they don't stay there; corticosteroids injected into joints are absorbed into the horse's system. Thus, joint injections with corticosteroids at least have the potential for causing systemic side effects such as laminitis, especially if multiple joints are injected at the same time. (Laminitis, an inflammatory condition of the horse's foot, is an uncommon side effect of corticosteroid use in horses.) Like any drug, corticosteroids certainly should not be used indiscriminately; the same can be said for any drug, however.

A full evaluation of all the effects, good and bad, of corticosteroid agents has not been completed and probably won't be for quite a while. The effects and side effects of corticosteroid injections seem to be related to variables such as the total dose given, how long each particular drug lasts in the joint, how often the joint is treated and which drug is used. It may be that the doses of corticosteroid agents currently used to treat inflamed joints are higher than what is actually needed to achieve the desired anti-inflammatory effect. Decreased doses will most likely decrease the potential for adverse side effects. However, even though there is much work to be done in evaluating corticosteroid agents in the treatment of arthritis in the horse, they are likely to remain first-line treatments in the fight against both acute and chronic arthritis for a long time to come.

## Non-steroidal Anti-inflammatory Drugs

Ancient medical practitioners knew that the chewing of willow bark could help relieve pain, fever and inflammation. In 1823, the active ingredient in willow bark was isolated and named salicin. In 1899, a derivative of salicin, acetylsalicylic acid, was made available for the first time. Acetylsalicylic acid is also called aspirin. Aspirin was the first in a line of many pharmaceuticals that are classified as non-steroidal anti-inflammatory drugs.

Non-steroidal anti-inflammatory drugs (NSAIDs) are unquestionably among the oldest and most frequently used medications for the treatment and control of arthritis in the horse. They are called non-steroidal because their chemical structure is different from that of the corticosteroid drugs that are also anti-inflammatory. They are a popular first-line systemic treatment for acute arthritis for the control of the pain and inflammation associated with that condition. NSAIDs are commonly given on a long-term basis to horses with osteoarthritis in an attempt to help them live and function with their chronic pain.

NSAIDs work by blocking the production of chemicals associated with the pain and inflammation, although the complete method of action of these drugs is not completely understood. There are many different steps in the chemical process at which the production of the chemicals can be blocked; thus, there are many different NSAIDs that work at the various steps. Since the different drugs work at different sites, they can have slightly different effects, too.

The most commonly prescribed NSAID is phenylbutazone (commonly known as bute). It's used so much because it's relatively inexpensive, at least when compared with other NSAIDs; it's fairly safe; and it's pretty effective. Over time, bute has proved its worth in the treatment of pain, fever and inflammation. Other commonly administered NSAIDs include aspirin, flunixin meglumine, meclofenamic acid, ketoprofen and naproxen.

NSAIDs are generally remarkably safe and effective drugs, but many myths and misconceptions about their effects and side effects abound. Bute is not a very potent pain reliever; its effects are similar to those of aspirin, another drug from the same class. You won't stop or mask the pain of a serious injury by giving a horse bute. Although side effects such as ulcers of the mouth and gastrointestinal tract and kidney problems have been reported using NSAIDs, they are *exceedingly* rare as long as you follow the prescribed doses for the drugs. Phenylbutazone seems to be the particular target of people's fears. While it's true that side effects may be seen in as little as a week if you merely double the recommended dose of bute, you shouldn't ever exceed the recommended dosage of *any* drug (other NSAIDs have a wider margin of safety; that is, higher doses than recommended seem to be better tolerated). Furthermore, if you want to get more pain-relieving effect than can be obtained with a single dose of one NSAID, don't give the horse an additional dose of a different NSAID thinking that you can avoid any side effects that might come from over-dosing the one; the effects *and* side effects of NSAIDs are cumulative.

If one NSAID doesn't seem to be effective for your horse, try another; since the drugs work in different ways, some horses may respond better to one drug from the class than another. As with any drug, NSAIDs should be used in a safe and effective dose according to what is specified by your veterinarian.

## Hyaluronan (Hyaluronic Acid)

As you remember, hyaluronan is a proteoglycan that's an important component of both the joint fluid and the joint cartilage. Its primary functions in the joint are involved in lubrication of both the soft tissues of the joint capsule and the cartilage itself.

The idea behind using hyaluronan to treat joint disease must not have been hard to come up with (it hasn't been used that long: only since 1970). It's been shown that joint inflammation tends to decrease the hyaluronan content of the joint. What could be a more obvious treatment than to put some more of the stuff back into the joint?

Behind that deceptively simple treatment concept lurks a lot of discussion about how and why hyaluronan works. Hyaluronan may have some short-term effect as a lubricant when it's injected into joints. However, given that it only stays in the joint for a matter of a few days, this is unlikely to be its most important effect. Of more interest and significance are the effects of hyaluronan as an anti-inflammatory agent and as a substance that may promote the production of normal joint fluid.

It's been well demonstrated that hyaluronan is anti-inflammatory. Some of these anti-inflammatory properties relate to the fact that hyaluronan is a rather large molecule; it's sheer size from a molecular standpoint may help keep other molecules out of the joint (this phenomenon is called steric hindrance). Hyaluronan also acts to inhibit some of the cells that are released into the joint during the inflammatory process. Hyaluronan is also frequently combined with corticosteroids and injected into joints. A couple of studies have shown a more potent anti-inflammatory effect of the combination than when either product is used by itself.

Other studies have suggested that inflamed joint cells, cells that normally produce an abnormal joint fluid, can be stimulated to produce a more normal joint fluid when they are put in the presence of hyaluronan. The reason for this effect isn't known. Furthermore, the effect has only been shown in the test tube and not in the live horse. Still, it is an interesting potential benefit of treatment.

There are many hyaluronan products available for the treatment of joint disease in the horse. The biggest difference between them seems to be the molecular weight of the hyaluronan in the bottle (and the cost; the higher the molecular weight, the higher the cost). There's quite a bit of discussion about the effect of molecular weight; as with a lot of things, some people say that more is better, but there's not much evidence to support that claim. According to the reports in the veterinary literature, there seems to be little difference in the clinical response between horses treated with hyaluronan products of varying molecular weights (although this opinion may vary between individuals who treat joints).

What's really interesting about hyaluronan is that it may not even need to be injected directly into the joint to be effective. One study has shown that an intravenous form of hyaluronan is effective as an anti-inflammatory agent. Furthermore, the anti-inflammatory effect lasted for up to fifty days after injection even though it only stays in the bloodstream for a matter of minutes! Even though nobody knows exactly how IV hyaluronan works, it appears that, in addition to its anti-inflammatory effects, the drug may stimulate certain cells to produce hyaluronan in the joint. These are the same effects that may be seen when hyaluronan is injected directly into the joint; IV hyaluronan may be an even more effective way than local injection to stimulate the target cells.

Currently, hyaluronan therapy seems most effective for mild to moderate inflammation of the joint capsule and synovial membrane. It seems to be somewhat less effective when significant disease of the bone and cartilage is present (as in osteoarthritis). The IV form of hyaluronan is being increasingly used in place of the product injected in the joint because of its convenience; additionally, some veterinarians think that it is more effective when given that way.

## Polysulfated Glycosaminoglycan (Adequan)

The proteoglycans of the normal joint are a complex molecule made up of two parts. The core of the proteoglycan is protein; attached to the protein core is a chemical compound called a glycosaminoglycan (the compound is often abbreviated GAG). Glycosaminoglycans come in many different chemical shapes and sizes.

Polysulfated (this is just a chemical term that refers to how the molecule is put together) glycosaminoglycans are a group of drugs that have been around for only about thirty years. It's abbreviated PSGAG; in the United States PSGAG is marketed under the trade name of

Adequan; another, somewhat different drug with similar effects called Pentosan is also available in other countries. They were originally supposed to be used to treat diseases of the blood vessels; however, during the initial investigations of the drug, it was noted that it had an anti-inflammatory effect on joints. In addition, it was felt that the drug might help promote beneficial metabolic activity within joints, such as increased production of the proteoglycan components of the cartilage. Initially, the drug was marketed in Europe as a treatment for arthritis of the human knee; in the mid-1980s it became available for use in horses.

The GAG that gets polysulfated to make these drugs is chondroitin sulfate. Chondroitin 4–sulfate is the primary GAG that makes up the proteoglycans found in the joint cartilage. Human and animal studies (some of which have been done in horses) have suggested that chondroitin sulfate has anti-inflammatory effects in joints. In fact, PSGAG does appear to inhibit many of the harmful substances released during joint inflammation in test-tube situations.

Furthermore, there's some experimental work that shows that PSGAG also stimulates the production of hyaluronan in joints. PSGAG also appears to help stimulate the production of normal cartilage GAGs in some studies. This fact has been interpreted by some people to mean that PSGAG can actually protect a joint from damage and promote healing. That's quite a leap of faith; there are some conflicting results in this area. However, there are a lot of theoretical benefits to this stuff.

Practically, however, it's a little bit more difficult to evaluate how well PSGAGs actually work in joints. A study conducted in 1996 showed that most veterinarians were satisfied with PSGAG, but this was hardly a critical study of the effects of the drug. One problem with evaluating PSGAG is that nobody knows how the drug works; it's probably *not* due to its presence in the joint, since the drug appears to be rapidly cleared out of a joint after it gets there. However, at least in acutely inflamed joints, studies have shown that PSGAG has benefits in limiting inflammation. Also, many surgeons give a shot of PSGAG into joints upon which they've operated to help reduce inflammation and bleeding in the joint. (On the downside of this practice, the drug does appear to have the potential to suppress the infection-fighting immune system within a healing joint.)

The benefits of PSGAG are not nearly as obvious when they are used to treat chronic osteoarthritis. Decreasing inflammation in a joint with osteoarthritis is probably a good thing. However, it's not at all clear that there are any true effects from PSGAG insofar as protecting the joint cartilage or preventing further damage in a joint that is already damaged as some people have claimed. In fact, you could even argue that if a horse with osteoarthritis feels better because of decreased inflammation, he will be more likely to use the joint. This could ultimately make the problem worse more quickly.

There are two forms of PSGAG. One is given directly into the joint; the other is given in the muscle. Because of some reports of horses developing very sore joints after receiving PSGAG injections into them, the muscle shot has gained wide popularity. It's also a lot easier to give that way. However, the effects of the direct injection into the joint seem, according to the research, to be somewhat more consistent insofar as decreasing inflammation.

## Oral Joint Supplements

If you've been into a tack store lately, you may have noticed that something approaching two-thirds of the store is devoted to oral supplements meant to combat the bad effects of arthritis. The products are wonderfully packaged, heavily advertised, impressively endorsed and sometimes even recommended by veterinarians. That being said, at this point in time, no one knows how or if they work in horses.

Oral joint supplements usually contain at least one of four substances:

1.  Chondroitin sulfate is the primary GAG found in the hyaline cartilage of joints.

2.  Glucosamine is a sugar molecule from which the proteoglycans that are found in normal joint cartilage is made. It's actually found almost universally in small amounts in most foods (and in larger amounts in foods that contain cartilage). Glucosamine can be chemically constructed in several ways; glucosamine hydrochloride is one common form that's found in many equine products.

3.  Manganese is a trace mineral that, among its other functions, is used by the body to make glycosaminoglycans (GAG).

4.  Ascorbate has an essential role in the formation of the collagen fibers of normal joint cartilage.

Experimentally, orally administered chondroitin sulfate has been shown to have some anti-inflammatory effects in some species including humans but not yet in the horse. On the other hand, at least one human study showed that chondroitin sulfate isn't absorbed intact from the intestinal tract and that any direct action of chondroitin sulfate on the joint cartilage was impossible. (The word *intact* is important here; whether the intact molecule or just a portion of it is needed for chondroitin sulfate to be effective is another thing that isn't known.) Absorption studies on horses haven't been published yet but are being conducted. However, from all the studies that have been published, one thing seems certain with chondroitin sulfate: it seems incapable of hurting a horse.

Glucosamine is a complex sugar molecule from which the proteoglycans of normal joint cartilage are made. It's actually found almost universally in small amounts in most foods and in larger amounts in foods that contain cartilage. Research done on people with osteoarthritis of the knee who took glucosamine orally showed that it was as effective as ibuprofen, a commonly used non-steroidal anti-inflammatory drug, at controlling the pain and soreness associated with the disease. Other studies have shown that glucosamine has a direct anti-inflammatory effect. Furthermore, there is evidence (in humans) that glucosamine is absorbed from the gastrointestinal tract.

Glucosamine also increases the production of GAGs by the joint cartilage in the test tube. This intriguing finding brings up the question of whether glucosamine could be used to help "restore" joint cartilage that has been damaged or to promote cartilage health by helping it to maintain itself. If it could do these things, there's no reason why every horse—indeed, every person—shouldn't be taking the stuff. However, even when you don't consider this aspect of glucosamine therapy, it has shown the most impressive results of the oral supplements used to treat arthritis so far.

To date, only a few studies have been performed looking at the ability of oral joint supplements to treat joint inflammation in a horse, however. In separate studies, horse knee joints were irritated by the injection of a foreign substance. One group of horses was treated by injection of intravenous hyaluronan, intramuscular PSGAG and another with a heavily advertised brand of oral joint supplement. The first two treatments helped relieve the signs of inflammation (the PSGAG seemed better). The oral joint supplement had no apparent effect. This study certainly isn't the final word about oral joint supplements, and it may not even be the best experimental model in which to investigate arthritis. For example, injecting an irritating substance into a joint certainly doesn't mimic the changes that occur in osteoarthritis. Nonetheless, the results of this study showed that two injectable products seemed to help relieve joint inflammation; the oral one didn't.

However, other studies evaluating oral joint supplements have been more promising. A pilot study evaluating the effects of the products in an osteoarthritis model showed clinical relief of lameness in two horses (although there were no apparent effects on the joint fluid). Another study evaluated the effects of an oral joint supplement on twenty-five horses with osteoarthritis. The treated horses showed statistically significant improvement in their condition, as measured by a decrease in the lameness score, decreased response to flexion testing and increased length of stride. The improvement was noted in just two weeks after the onset of therapy and continued to the end of the six-week study. A third, recently reported study showed the products had some effectiveness in improving the lameness in horses affected with navicular syndrome. These studies certainly suggest that there is a reason to evaluate these products in horses more fully.

Given the relative lack of research on horses, as a potential purchaser of glucosamine and/or chondroitin sulfate products, there are other questions that you should be asking. For example, one question might be, "Does the product that I'm buying contain what the label says it does?" According to research at the University of Maryland, the answer is, "Not necessarily." In fact, researchers at the university tested twenty-seven glucosamine or chondroitin-sulfate products and found that a number of them didn't have the amounts of the product in them that the label said they did. The actual content can even vary from month to month as different batches of product are released. (Unfortunately, the names of all of the products used in the Maryland study were not released.) You should call the company whose products you are considering purchasing and ask them how they control the purity of their products.

Furthermore, how do you know which product to choose? There's a lot of advertising hoohah about where the glucosamine and chondroitin sulfate found in these products come from. Some of the products are derived from the windpipe of a cow. Another product is made from shark cartilage (the fact that the product comes from shark cartilage offers some distinctive packaging opportunities, when compared to those offered by products derived from cows). Yet another product comes from sea mussels (and smells like it, too). Sea mussels and shark cartilage don't have glucosamine in them; that has to be added (the source of glucosamine is ground-up crab shells). At this point in time, it's not clear that the source of your horse's glucosamine and chondroitin sulfate makes any difference whatsoever, as long it is from a high-quality, purified source. And again, most of these products are not rigorously tested for the actual content of their active ingredients.

Should you use oral joint supplement products to help treat or prevent arthritis problems in your horse? At this time, there's no clear answer to that question. Research does seem to indicate that chondroitin sulfate and glucosamine do have some promising anti-inflammatory and joint protective effects, particularly if used early in the treatment of arthritis. There's no question that the supplements don't seem to be able to hurt your horse (your pocketbook is another matter). There's also no question that many people (including veterinarians) recommend them. But there's also no evidence to date that they are consistently effective in relieving inflammation or promoting cartilage maintenance in horses or in any other species. However, oral joint supplements are almost certain *not* to work in horses with advanced osteoarthritis, since these horses may not have much cartilage left to restore. Further muddying the waters is the fact that no dosages of these products have been established.

Is all this hubbub about oral joint supplements confusing to you? Well, it should be. These products are frequently marketed as a nutritional supplement with implied medical benefits. Even the word "nutraceutical" (combining "nutrition" and "pharmaceutical") that is used to describe these and other products only adds to the confusion because there is, as yet, no generally accepted definition for the term. Medical products fall under the jurisdiction of the U.S. Food and Drug

Administration; nutritional supplements don't. Medical products have to be rigorously tested, must be labeled properly and have to show evidence of effectiveness; nutritional supplements don't.

Ultimately, the only way that the buying public is going to find out if oral joint supplements are effective treatments for arthritis is to demand that some sort of standards for the production of these products be followed. For example, manufacturers could be required to follow the regulations governing good manufacturing practices, so that as a purchaser of the products, you could be assured of their quality. Another option might be the newly established North American Nutraceutical Council. This group was established to put checks and balances on the industry of nutritional supplements that claim to be of health benefit to animals, in hopes of protecting both animals and their owners. Alternatively, the FDA could get in and classify these substances as drugs and monitor them accordingly; however, this would require much more stringent standards that might render these potentially useful products unavailable.

Until *some* standard is adopted, you will not be sure that all of the oral joint supplement products that you can potentially purchase are properly labeled, adequately tested and reasonably effective. Until then, and until further investigations are completed, the answer to the question of whether these supplements are an important weapon in the war against arthritis in your horse or just another opportunity for you to spend money on him is going to be largely a matter of guesswork, trial and error.

## Superoxide Dismutase

Superoxide dismutase is one of a group of chemicals that pick up and remove free-radical compounds that are generated during joint inflammation. Free radicals cause cell death and destruction and resultant tissue damage. Obviously, something that would remove free radicals would be of potential benefit in the treatment of arthritis.

So far, the actual effects of superoxide dismutase therapy are poorly understood; however, the therapy is fairly new. The compounds are purely anti-inflammatory and have no direct pain-relieving effect. There are oral preparations of the stuff that can be purchased over the counter; there is a veterinary preparation (called orgotein; the trade name is Palosein) that is given by injection in the muscle. (A number of years ago, Palosein was injected directly into joints, where it promptly caused tremendous inflammation. As a result, no one uses it that way anymore.) The response to the drug in clinical tests for the treatment of traumatic arthritis and other conditions has been variable. As a cautionary note, allergic reactions to orgotein injections have been occasionally reported.

## MIA (Sodium Moniodoacetate)

MIA is a toxic chemical that destroys joint cartilage. It was initially used as a method of causing inflammation in joints so as to perform experimental investigations on arthritis. Obviously, this is not a substance that you want to go about injecting willy-nilly into joints.

However, in the spirit of making plowshares out of swords, a veterinarian working at The Ohio State University decided to see if the chemical could be used to destroy joint cartilage and cause joints that had been damaged by arthritis to fuse. (The surgical way to perform joint fusion, called arthrodesis, is discussed in the next chapter.) He injected MIA into the lower hock joints of horses and found that some fusion did occur. He then injected horses with arthritis of the lower hock joints (bone spavin) with the MIA and found some good success as well. In fact, studies have shown a better than 70 percent success rate in fusing arthritic hock joints with MIA (success being measured as a return to athletic function). Figure 7 shows an example of fused joints.

· Figure 7 ·

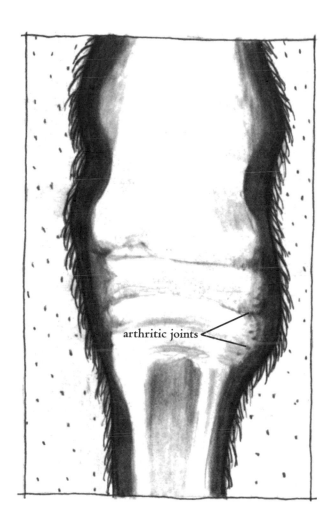

*When arthritis of the lower hock joints (bone spavin) occurs,*
*fusion with injections of MIA is an experimental option.*

The success of MIA injections in treating the lower hock joints is due to the fact that they can be fused with no ill effect to the horse, since these joints don't move very much anyway. MIA injections have also been tried in an effort to fuse arthritic pastern joints (ringbone), with much more limited experiences and successes.

There are some significant downsides to consider about MIA therapy, however. First of all, MIA is not licensed for any sort of medical use. Thus, the veterinarian who uses it and the owner who allows it to be used are proceeding at their own risk. Second, there are some nasty complications that can occur as a result of MIA injections, some of which are fatal. These complications usually result from the chemical leaking into joints where it doesn't belong or from breakdown and instability of the joint after injection (especially in the pastern). This is not the sort of therapy that should be considered lightly. Surgical alternatives are available to MIA fusion (but there's no guarantee that they will work, either).

## JOINT PROTECTION?

You are learning that there's no sure-fire treatment for every case of arthritis, especially since the term arthritis can imply so many things. Without doubt, you've heard that an ounce of prevention is worth a pound of cure. Thus, one of the big questions out there for medicine is, "Can joints be protected from wear and tear and arthritis thus be prevented?" (Obviously, you can't prevent joint damage from things like acute accidents; horses will go on hurting themselves forever.)

Given all of the real and proposed anti-inflammatory and cartilage metabolism-promoting benefits of such substances as oral joint supplements, PSGAG and hyaluronan, it certainly is seductive to think that if you could provide those benefits before joint problems happen, you could have a much greater chance of keeping your horse free of arthritis. It is possible that these drugs may be able to help the horse's joints recover more quickly from the minor injuries that exercise-induced trauma may do to them. There's certainly no question that the PSGAG and hyaluronan are currently used in an effort to prevent joint problems, particularly in high-performance horses. The value of the horses participating in racing, jumping and cutting and the potential financial rewards to the winners of the competitions means that no potential stone that can provide a competitive "edge" will remain unturned, whether or not there is any demonstrable benefit from the stone turning.

At this point in time, the use of these drugs in this fashion precedes any real scientific data that they can be effective. However, given the realities of such things as bad conformation, accidental joint trauma and the heavy and frequently unnatural work that is asked of horses (such activities as jumping, passage and running at a gallop for miles are not done on a regular basis by horses in the wild), it does seem unrealistic to think that giving drugs to otherwise healthy horses will prevent *any* cases of arthritis from ever developing. In fact, the question of whether drugs can prevent cases of joint disease will probably never be answered satisfactorily. It would take a whole lot of time, effort and money to try to conduct a study that might answer the question. At this point, the answer, "Can't hurt; might help," seems to be good enough for many horse people who wonder whether joints can be protected by giving medication to the healthy horse.

# CHAPTER 6

# Surgical Treatments for Arthritis

Much as with medical therapy, the success of surgical therapy for arthritis largely depends on the problem that you are treating. The worse the injury to the joint, the less likely it is that the horse will be able to return to his full, normal function. In selected cases, however, surgery does offer a permanent solution to an arthritis problem and allows for a return to normal function of a joint that was previously affected with either chronic or acute arthritis.

## LAVAGE

To lavage a joint means to rinse it out. The procedure is done using sterile saltwater solutions; sometimes antibiotics are added to the saltwater. Rinsing out a joint that's filled with inflammatory chemicals has some obvious benefits. Lavage helps remove the harmful chemicals that are released during the inflammatory process, and it can help protect the joint from the damage these chemicals cause. Lavage is usually considered as a treatment option for things like acute arthritis, joint trauma (to remove blood from the joint or to clean out a joint that has sustained a wound prior to sewing it up) and joint infections (lavage is an important way by which the infective bacteria are removed from the joint).

Joint lavage can be done in the standing horse through a needle. The joint is filled up with fluid; then the fluid is released, along with the contents of the joint. This is done several times to try to get the most complete rinse possible.

Lavage through a single needle is not the ideal type of lavage, however. A better job can be done if two needles are placed in a joint; fluid can be pumped into the joint via one needle and released out of the other. The so-called through-and-through lavage that this allows is more complete than that which can be obtained through a single needle. However, the best lavage for a joint is obtained via the arthroscope.

## ARTHROSCOPY

As mentioned in the previous chapter, the advent of surgical arthroscopy has been truly revolutionary in the treatment of horse joints. By now, no one needs to be convinced that when it can be used, arthroscopy offers tremendous advantages over cutting open the joint capsule and mucking around in the joint. These advantages include:

1. Less tissue damage to the joint that's being operated on.
2. Increased accuracy in the diagnosis of joint problems. You can actually see the joint better using an arthroscope than when opening up the joint capsule.
3. More efficient removal of joint debris and inflammatory by-products due to the continuous rinsing of the joint (lavage) that goes on during arthroscopic surgery.
4. The ability to operate on more than one joint during a single surgery, if necessary.

5. Decreased pain after surgery.

6. A better cosmetic appearance to the joint after surgery.

7. A quicker return to function of the horse who has had surgery (when compared with opening up the joint).

8. Most importantly, the post-operative results are better with arthroscopy than with opening up the joint capsule!

The surgical technique for arthroscopy is amazingly simple. First, the joint is filled up with a sterile saline, or other saltwater, solution. This stretches out the joint so that you can stick in the arthroscope without hurting other structures. A small hole is made in the skin and joint capsule so that the arthroscope can be placed in the joint; another small hole is made at some other location in the joint so that surgical instruments to do the work can be placed. Sterile saline is flushed through the arthroscope as needed to keep things clean and clear inside the joint. The surgeon then works away using the arthroscope to look around, usually with a camera attached to it so he or she doesn't have to be bending over and looking into the scope all the time, and the instruments to do whatever work is needed in the joint. After the surgery is done, a few stitches are placed in the skin, the limb is bandaged, and the horse is hopefully on its way to recovery!

# SURGERY FOR JOINT FRACTURES

Arthroscopy is the surgical technique of choice for removing the chips and chunks that break off the bones of racing horses. It can also be used to repair "slab" fractures of the racing horse's knee (they are called slab fractures because a slab of bone breaks off one of the six cube-shaped bones that make up the knee joint). Any time that you can minimize the surgical trauma that you do to a joint already traumatized by injury by using an arthroscope, you should take advantage of the opportunity.

For more extensive fractures that involve the joint surfaces, more extensive repairs are needed. These repairs involve putting back together the jigsaw puzzle of fractured pieces of bone using stainless-steel screws, plates and/or wires. Obviously, these are advanced surgical techniques that need to be performed by specially trained surgeons in hospital situations. Still, many horses with fractures that go into joints can be saved, and some can even return to full function.

Assuming that the fracture is not so bad as to preclude repair, the limiting factor for return of a horse with a fracture into the joint to full function is the amount of damage to the joint cartilage. As you recall, cartilage doesn't heal. Thus, in order to get the horse back to work, the cartilage surfaces have to be reconstructed as precisely as possible. The surgeon tries to rebuild the joint surface so that it is as smooth as possible; he or she doesn't want any steps or bumps where the cartilage from one bone comes in contact with another.

To the degree that the surgeon can realign the joint surfaces, a repair of a fracture into a joint will be more or less successful. If the repair is precise and the fracture is relatively simple to fix, the horse may even be able to return to the level of performance that he was participating in prior to his injury. If, however, there are many pieces of bone to try to put back together, it's pretty much impossible to reconstruct the joint surfaces. Such a surgery can be like trying to nail a piece of Jell-O to a tree. If the joint surface can't be put back together, it will serve as a source of irritation and inflammation for the joint, the horse will most likely be lame after surgery and osteoarthritis will develop in the joint.

# ARTHRODESIS (JOINT FUSION)

Surgical arthrodesis of a joint results in the complete destruction of a joint. The idea is to destroy the joint that has been affected by chronic inflammation or acute trauma and convert it into a single bone. To perform the technique, the cartilage in the joint to be fused is removed by the surgeon, and the bones on each side of the joint are pushed together, usually using bone screws or plates to keep the bones in place (Figure 8). Bone grows together across the former joint space, and the two bones become one.

Depending on which joint is fused (and the success of the surgery), the horse who has had a surgical arthrodesis may limp forever or be completely sound. This depends directly on the normal range of motion on the joint that is to be fused. For example, if a horse sustains a severe injury to his fetlock joint, it is sometimes possible to salvage him by fusing the joint. The fetlock joint normally has a tremendous range of motion. If, by fusing the joint, you eliminate the normal motion, the horse will forever walk around stiff-legged. While this is certainly not desirable for a horse who needs to perform some athletic function, it may be perfectly acceptable for a horse who is only going to be used for breeding or is only going to be kept in pasture as a pet.

In two situations, however, fusion of the affected joints can sometimes result in a permanent cure for lameness. The small bones of the lower hock and the two bones that make up the horse's pastern joint normally have virtually no range of motion. Thus, when the pastern or lower hock joints are affected by arthritis (ringbone and bone spavin, respectively) and/or injury, it's sometimes possible to perform an arthrodesis, stop the motion across the diseased joint, eliminate the pain of arthritis and return the horse to full athletic soundness.

Surgical arthrodesis is anything but a piece of cake. Not all surgeries are successful. Not only that, it's pretty expensive. Before considering this option to treat your horse's injury or arthritic condition, spend a lot of time with your veterinarian and/or the surgeon who wants to perform the surgery to find out if this is a viable treatment option.

· FIGURE 8 ·

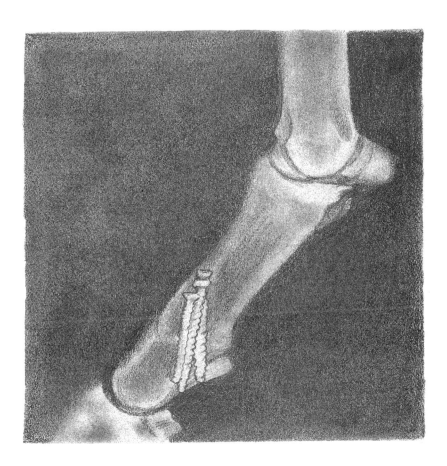

*Bone screws have been placed across the pastern joint of this horse to cause fusion.*

# JOINT RESURFACING

One of the most active areas of current arthritis research involves the resurfacing of the joint cartilage. Horses are too big and put too much stress on their joints for replacing arthritic joints with plastic ones, as is done in human surgery. Thus, a number of experimental techniques to replace areas of damaged cartilage with cartilage grafts have been tried. Unfortunately, so far, the results of the tests have indicated early promise, with the grafted areas of the joint looking good a few months after they are resurfaced, with disappointing longer-term results (the grafts ultimately fail). Obviously, if joint-resurfacing techniques could ever be developed, the potential benefits to the horse (and human) population would be almost unimaginable. That's why researchers keep plugging away in hopes of finding a surgical solution to the problem of arthritis.

# CHAPTER 7

# Alternative Therapies for Arthritis

Before attempting to tackle the numerous types of therapies grouped together as "alternatives" to "traditional" medicine, the author would like to take a moment to discuss some medical philosophy. One of the real strengths of traditional medicine is its willingness, even eagerness, to question itself. Doctors are constantly looking for evidence that particular treatments work. They are constantly rejecting treatments that have been shown not to work. For doctors to be inclined to accept any form of treatment as legitimate, however, they want hard evidence that it is effective. Good doctors constantly adapt and improve their skills to incorporate treatments for conditions that are better than what has come before. Good doctors want their patients to get better using *whatever* treatment will get that patient there. But before prescribing such a treatment, they want to have confidence that it might work. A doctor has his or her reputation at stake when prescribing a treatment. Before putting his or her reputation on the line by recommending a therapy, he or she should reasonably expect to have some sort of proof that the treatment works.

It is to be hoped that all of those who participate in a medical field ultimately do so because they want to make their patients better. Unfortunately, the goal of making every patient better, while laudable, is also impossible. If any sort of therapy could be demonstrated to be *the* answer to a particular problem, there would be no need for any alternative therapy. Everyone would just use the one that worked all the time. It would be absolutely pointless to do otherwise.

Doctors generally understand this. Unfortunately, patients often do not. Many times (and particularly in some cases of osteoarthritis) there is no solution that always works; sometimes there is no solution that *ever* works. The answer "There's nothing more that can be done" is often considered to be as unacceptable by a patient as it is frustrating to the doctor who says it. This is perfectly understandable; no one wants to give up hope. However, as a result, patients with conditions that do not have solutions offered to them from one area of medicine or who are scared of the solutions that are offered frequently turn to another area in hopes of an alternative. Where there are alternatives, there is still hope.

That being said, one must also be aware of false hopes. As a point in fact, there is no known cure for osteoarthritis, in the horse or in any other species. Thus, any sort of alternative therapy that presents itself as a cure for osteoarthritis must be considered not an alternative but a hoax. That is not to say that some benefit may not be obtained from an alternative form of therapy, only that such therapies must be approached with an expectation of realistic results, not miracles.

Furthermore, before proceeding with an alternative therapy, it would be useful to have some sort of hard evidence that the therapy is effective. Unfortunately, for most forms of alternative therapy, that evidence just isn't there. Glowing testimonials from friends and paid endorsements from riders and trainers are not a substitute for scientific data. In many cases of acute arthritis, horses will get better no matter what form of therapy they receive. Spontaneous resolution of a problem or temporary relief from chronic signs is typical of many diseases. Just because the improvement in the horse's condition followed treatment doesn't mean that the treatment caused the improvement; if "b" follows "a," it doesn't mean "a" caused "b."

For example, hundreds of years ago it was thought that flies ("b") arose spontaneously from decomposing meat ("a"). This belief was not challenged until someone put a piece of meat in a jar and covered it with cheesecloth. The meat still decomposed; however, no flies arose. In medicine, when something happens or when a problem resolves itself spontaneously, it's not at all uncommon for credit (or blame) to be given somewhere it isn't due.

You should also be aware that not all of the alternative therapies for arthritis (or any other condition) are practiced by people who are licensed or trained. You should be very careful of individuals who promote or practice a therapy and who don't have a veterinary degree or aren't referred by a veterinarian. You should be particularly careful if that individual objects to working along with your veterinarian. Alternative therapies seem to be enjoying an increasing popularity, and there is very little actual knowledge about the pluses and minuses of them; thus, the horse owner, who is concerned only with helping the horse, is something of an easy target for someone who is intent on selling him- or herself under the guise of helping, too.

If you are not satisfied with your horse's response to traditional medical options and you choose to pursue alternative forms of therapy, try to approach them with a healthy skepticism. Look for proof that something works before you go and dump lots of money into it. Try to evaluate a response to a therapy with your head and not your heart. Keep your fingers crossed and hope for the best. Everyone is looking to help horses (and every other mammalian species) with arthritis. If you find something that seems to help in the treatment of your horse's arthritis, don't keep it under your hat. Perhaps someday, everyone else will be able to benefit from it, too.

# ACUPUNCTURE

Acupuncture is based on a philosophy of medicine that is in many ways completely different from traditional Western medicine. People who perform acupuncture place needles, injections of various solutions, laser light and even implants at certain points on the horse's body. By doing so, acupuncturists are trying to stimulate *qi* (pronounced "chee"), or energy. The various traditional acupuncture points are supposed to relate to different body organs and body functions. Stimulation of the acupuncture points by one of the various methods is supposed to help the body's defenses fight illnesses, help the body heal and to relieve pain. Although it hasn't yet been shown that acupuncture can help fight illness or improve healing in horses, there have been some reports of success with acupuncture in relieving pain, especially back pain, in the horse.

Early pilot studies in horses suggested that acupuncture might help relieve the pain that causes lameness. A few poorly designed trials confirmed this notion. But one of the very few properly designed trials of acupuncture in horses showed that acupuncture-treated horses did no better than untreated controls. This trend has been seen in human studies, as well, where the more rigorous the experimental design of the study, the less likely that an effect from acupuncture will be seen. Skeptics note that a painful stimulus at one point in the body is well-known to cause a decrease in pain at another and that pain from any source tends to come and go.

Acupuncture isn't something to be done casually. Since it uses needles and injections, acupuncture should be regarded as a form of surgery. It should only be done by people trained in its use and application; ideally, that person is a veterinarian with an interest in acupuncture. For more information about acupuncture, you can contact the International Veterinary Acupuncture Society, 2140 Conestoga Road, Chester Springs, PA 19425, or phone (215) 827-7245.

## CHIROPRACTIC

Chiropractic is based on the belief that the vertebrae of the spinal column, when not in correct position, can cause pain and dysfunction of various parts of the horse's body. One way this dysfunction could conceivably show up is with joint pain. Chiropractors try to manipulate the horse's body so as to "readjust" the perceived misalignments of the spinal column. Even in human medicine, misalignments of the spine have never been shown to exist.

Many questions need to be answered before chiropractic will be considered as a valid therapeutic modality by the veterinary community. For example, no one has ever published a study showing that it is effective; no one has ever published a paper showing how a diagnosis is achieved; no one has ever published a paper showing that the horse's vertebrae can even be manipulated. Furthermore, there are neither educational nor licensing requirements for practitioners of veterinary chiropractic. None of this appears to have dented its popularity, however.

Should you choose to employ chiropractic for your horse, at least try to find someone who:

1. Is a veterinarian and has training and expertise in animal anatomy and physiology.

93

2. Doesn't use things like mallets and boards to bang on the horse's back (and cause potential injury).

3. Has been trained by the American Veterinary Chiropractic Association, P.O. Box 249, Port Byron, IL 62441, phone (309) 523-3995.

# ULTRASOUND

Therapeutic ultrasound (as opposed to the diagnostic ultrasound that is used to evaluate injuries) is a popular form of treatment that has been used for the past fifty years or so by human physical therapists in rehabilitation of some types of injuries. Ultrasound is a sound wave that penetrates tissue and causes heat to be produced in it. In humans, this can have some beneficial effects insofar as helping to relieve muscle and joint pain and soreness and decrease swelling. Ultrasound can also be used with medications applied on top of the treated area; it's hoped that the ultrasound will help the medications penetrate the skin and get to the problem.

There aren't any studies on the effectiveness of ultrasound as a treatment for arthritis in horses. Nor are there studies about the effects of different frequencies of the sound waves used for treatment or the length of time that treatment should continue. Ultrasound would certainly not be indicated in the treatment of acute arthritis; adding heat to an already inflamed area would certainly have the potential to make the problem worse. Still, ultrasound appears to have little potential to cause any harm to an osteoarthritic joint; its biggest drawback is the expense of treatment. Some veterinarians recommend the use of ultrasound in treating joint stiffness or in helping to decrease joint stiffness after surgery.

# HERBAL AND NATURAL THERAPIES

For some people, the word *natural* is a synonym for "better." That's not always the case, though. In fact, humans have had a long history of natural therapies. Prior to the advent of modern medicine, natural therapy was all that was available. You lived a short life, you had lots of kids in hopes that a few of them would survive, and you used whatever you could find to help fight disease and infections. On the other hand, taking an "unnatural" substance such as an antibiotic does seem to be a reasonable alternative to the "natural" option of death from an aggressive infection. Obviously, natural is not necessarily better; it's just an alternative.

Still, it's an undeniable fact that many currently available medications are derived from plant and other natural substances and that these substances can be used to treat diseases, including arthritis. Such substances as arnica, Saint-John's wort and marigold have been used to treat such things as sprains and bruises for literally hundreds of years. However, it's important to remember that the amounts of the substances contained in natural medicines are not rigorously controlled, nor have many of them been studied for their effectiveness. In fact, yucca, a natural substance from a cactus plant that is frequently combined with anise (the stuff that gives black licorice its distinctive taste) in products sold over the counter for the treatment of arthritis, does not appear to have any definable effect in the treatment of arthritis, according to *texts* on herbal pharmacy.

Of course, some forms of "natural" therapies don't use foreign substances at all; therapies such as heat, cold or water could all be considered natural (and are used by practitioners of traditional medicine, too). People who promote and use natural therapies to treat arthritis should have extensive training in them and should either be or work closely with veterinarians.

# HOMEOPATHY

Homeopathic treatment is based on the idea that if some of a thing is bad, less is great (really). This line of treatment, which was started in the 1700s, relies on the premise that the "essence" of substances, some of which are quite harmful, have beneficial effects in treating disease and in stimulating the body's natural defenses. Essences are obtained by diluting the substances that are used for treatment to the point that they can't even be measured (the substances are so dilute that they literally don't exist); these dilutions are then used for treatment. There's absolutely no good information out there about the effects of homeopathy in the treatment of equine arthritis; however, the whole concept of treatment of disease conditions with essences of things that are no longer there is one that is at odds with any legitimate science. (Imagine trying to run your car on the essence of gasoline!)

# MAGNETS

You can strap magnets onto just about any area of the horse, thanks to pads, boots and blankets that have been designed for this purpose. You can buy machines that create a magnetic field that pulses on and off. Magnets have been tried as therapy since at least the 1600s. So far, no one has shown that they do anything.

Machines that pulse magnetic fields are approved by the U.S. Food and Drug Association for the treatment of delayed and non-union bone fractures. The pulsing field is able to cause a small electrical voltage in tissue; the effects of the machines are thought to be electrical, not magnetic. Their use in the treatment of fresh fractures, wound and soft-tissue healing is the subject of ongoing investigation; the devices may have limited use in these areas. Some studies even show that the machines are detrimental to the healing of fresh fractures. Unfortunately, the principal use of the machines in people (delayed fractures) is not one that appears often in horses.

There is no known biologic mechanism by which applying a static magnetic field (one that doesn't change) to tissue could have an effect. Magnetic devices have been advertised for a long time as having all sorts of purported benefits, mostly involving their proposed ability to increase circulation to an area (you could buy magnetic insoles for your boots from the Sears catalog in the 1800s). Blood is good; without blood, tissue dies. One hope with magnets is that by increasing the flow of blood to an area, healing will be promoted. This has never been conclusively demonstrated; one study that was done using magnets suggested an increase in bone activity under magnetic pads applied to the cannon bone, but that study has been roundly criticized in scientific circles. However, even if magnets were to increase circulation to any area, it's never been demonstrated that increasing circulation to an area would decrease the amount of time that it would take to return injured tissue to normal. In fact, increasing circulation to an already inflamed joint would probably not be a good thing, just as increasing bone activity in a joint with osteoarthritis in which increased bone activity in the joint is part of the problem would be bad. Furthermore, in some chronic inflammatory conditions, increased circulation actually becomes a problem in its own right.

There have been studies conducted on the effects of static magnetic fields on tissue for the last 100 years. The effects on various cells appear to depend on the amount of magnetism applied and the tissue examined. When effects of static magnetic fields have been seen, they are generated under intense fields that are hundreds of times stronger than the fields produced in the devices sold to horse owners. Unfortunately, at least when it comes to true science, static magnets have so far not been conclusively demonstrated to have any beneficial effect in the healing of anything (including arthritis). On the flip side, many people have voiced concerns about the effects of magnetic fields generated from electric power lines (those concerns haven't been substantiated either).

The bottom line with magnets and your horse's arthritis is that you can buy them, you can try them, but you certainly can't be sure if they are going to do anything to help. Unfortunately, the public seems to have little protection from medical devices that have no apparent benefit.

# LASER

Laser therapy employs concentrated light on the skin surface in an effort to stimulate healing. The purported effects of laser therapy are increasing circulation to the treated area. Laser therapy has also been used in an effort to stimulate the acupuncture points of the horse. As with magnets, little actual research into the effects of laser therapy on horses has been done; most good studies on laser therapy of arthritis in people have shown no effect.

Since there's virtually no scientific evidence to support the use of any of these therapeutic methods, you're left to rely on the experiences of your friends who may have tried them; the testimonials of people who may have been paid to support them; and the word of practitioners (who may have a vested interest in using or promoting them). In some cases, alternative therapies may have the potential to be effective, but they have not been proven to be effective so far. So what's the bottom line with alternative therapies for the treatment of arthritis? At the very least, it has to be "Buyer beware." At worst, such therapies are a continuation of the quackery that has plagued medical consumers for hundreds of years.

# CHAPTER 8

# Horseshoeing and Its Effects on Joints

ONE OF THE EASIEST THINGS (AND ONE OF THE ONLY things) about the horse that you can manipulate is the hoof. It's properly perceived that the hoof is an important structure. "No foot, no horse"; in fact, about 70 percent of all lameness is reported to arise from the hoof. In terms of the treatment of arthritis, adjustments and manipulations of the hoof are commonly made, particularly in the control and management of osteoarthritis. However, until recently, surprisingly little actual research has been done examining how shoeing affects the horse's leg. The results of the studies that have been done show that the effects of shoeing on horse legs are often different from what you would expect. They also show that you may be able to do less to affect a horse's joints with shoeing changes than you may think.

Most changes that are made on a horse's foot for the treatment of arthritis are done in an attempt to affect the way the horse strides. If, due to the pain and inflammation of arthritis, the horse is reluctant to stride, manipulations of the foot are performed in an effort to make it easier for the horse's foot to go forward. This is most commonly done by changing the foot length, the hoof angle and/or the type of shoe that is applied to the foot. The usual goal of these changes is to improve or ease the breakover of the horse's foot.

As the horse's leg comes back to the ground after moving through the air, it usually hits the ground heel first. As the horse moves forward, the weight moves forward from the heels over the toe on the front of the foot. Finally, the leg comes off the ground, and the whole sequence repeats itself. *Breakover* refers to the foot rolling over the front of the toe as the horse strides. The idea behind improving breakover is to make it easier for the horse to get his leg up off the ground. If the horse's leg hurts from arthritis of a joint, by making it easier to get his leg off the ground, he likely will be able to travel forward more easily.

It has been demonstrated that shoeing can affect how the horse's foot breaks over the toe. This is generally done in one of several ways. First, the length of the horse's foot can be shortened. It's been shown that as hoof length increases, the breakover tends to be delayed, and the leg is lifted higher off the ground as the horse strides forward. Of course, there are limits to how short you can make the horse's foot without making him sore.

Breakover may also be affected by the angle of the foot. The hoof angle is measured up the front of the hoof, usually using a measuring device made for this purpose. The normal hoof angle (which is usually between 50 and 55 degrees for a front foot and slightly steeper for a hind foot) can be raised either by shortening the toe of the foot or raising the heel. This can be acomplished either by trimming or by adding a horseshoe pad between the shoe and the foot. By making the hoof angle steeper, you sort of pitch the horse forward onto his toe and hopefully make him break over more quickly.

It's been well demonstrated that you can affect the breakover by changing the foot angle. The problem is, you can't do it consistently. That is, by changing the hoof angle, you are likely to cause some change in the horse's stride. But that change isn't consistent between horses, and it's not even consistent on the same horse at different gaits. This frustrating fact is probably predictable when you realize that research has also shown that changing the angle of the foot really doesn't affect the angles in the joints themselves all that much. For example, a change in the hoof angle of 10 degrees (which is a whole bunch) only changes the angle of the fetlock joint 1 degree and the angle of the pastern by 3 degrees. So, insofar as treating a horse with arthritis, if you try to make angle changes in the hoof to help him out, you may or may not get the effect that you are looking for.

Finally, the type of shoe that is applied to the horse's foot may affect the breakover. In an effort to improve breakover, the horse's toe may be squared off with a rasp; the shoe may be set well behind the toe; and/or a shoe with a rolled or "rocker" toe may be applied to the hoof (Figure 9). The actual changes to the horse's stride that these sorts of shoes cause have not been well-evaluated, however.

The bottom line with attempting to help your horse's arthritis by doing things to his feet is a bit frustrating. You may be able to help your horse stride more easily by trying to work on his feet; you may not. It's mostly a matter of trial and error (so don't think that your farrier or veterinarian is some sort of an idiot when shoeing changes don't seem to help). Shoeing changes for horses with arthritis are probably worth a try; just don't get your hopes up too high.

· Figure 9 ·

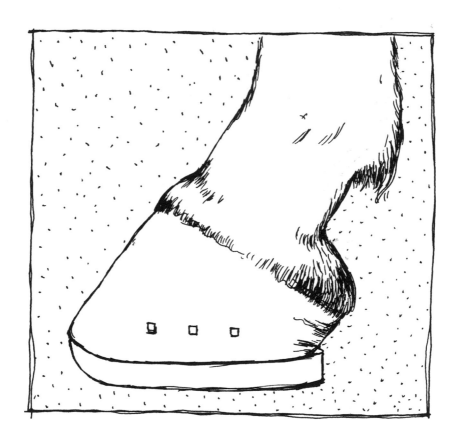

*A "rocker" toed horse shoe.*

# CHAPTER 9

# Special Situations: Osteochondrosis and Joint Infections

Arthritis is not limited to problems caused by joint trauma or overuse. Many other conditions can affect the joints of the horse and cause arthritis. Although there's not enough room in this book to discuss all of the conditions that affect horse joints, two conditions, osteochondrosis and joint infections, are important and occur frequently enough to merit discussion.

## OSTEOCHONDROSIS

Osteochondrosis (OC, for short) is a perplexing condition that is associated with arthritis in the joints of many mammalian species (including people and, of course, horses). The *-osis* of osteochondrosis is a medical suffix that merely indicates that a disease process is present; the *osteochondro-* part of the word means that the disease involves the bone (*osteo*) and cartilage (*chondro*). OC is an abnormality of the joint cartilage; sometimes this abnormality can even extend down into the supporting bone. The abnormality usually shows up on X-rays of an affected joint as either a chunk of cartilage that's not attached to the underlying bone or as a hole under the joint surface. It's been suggested that as many as 5 to 20 percent of all horses are affected by OC. Obviously, it's an important condition.

OC is perplexing because, at this time, nobody knows exactly what causes it. Many factors, such as nutrition, exercise, heredity and trauma, have been considered and are likely to contribute to the condition. To add to the confusion, from microscopic studies of joints affected with OC, it's also clear that not all horses who have a condition that can be described as a form of OC actually have the same underlying disease process going on. The chunks of cartilage found in the joints of some horses with OC clearly seem to come from areas in which the cartilage has developed abnormally; in others, the chunks appear to be normal bits of cartilage that simply break off from an apparently normal joint surface. Furthermore, OC is perplexing because not all horses with joints that are affected by OC seem to develop any clinical problems in them. Even the terminology used to describe the disease can add to the confusion; terms such as osteochondrosis, osteochondritis, osteochondritis dissecans and developmental orthopedic disease can all start to run together if you are trying to understand what's going on with this condition. (In fact, all of the preceding terms may be appropriate in certain instances; this section will try to help clear up a bit of this confusion.)

There's no question that OC is a disease that begins to show up in young horses as they develop and mature; thus OC is properly included as one of a group of diseases that are collectively referred to as "developmental orthopedic diseases." How and why particular individuals develop OC is still something of a mystery, however.

In some horses with OC, the joint cartilage appears to be normal. In others with OC, the joint cartilage in the affected joint doesn't develop in its customary fashion; it may be thicker than normal. If it's thicker, all of the cartilage cells in the area affected by OC may be unable to get enough nutrition from the joint fluid; thus some of the cartilage may be weaker than normal due to poor health. Alternatively, thickened cartilage may be structurally weaker than normal cartilage and thus be unable to stand up to the normal stresses that the weight of the horse puts on the joint. Yet another type of cartilage abnormality that still fits under the OC heading can be created by feeding diets that are lacking in copper.

It's usually not too hard to figure out when a horse is being bothered by OC. This sequence is fairly typical. OC causes an affected joint to become inflamed; a lameness examination determines which joint is affected with a problem; an X-ray determines that the problem is OC. If OC is the underlying problem, it may be reasonable to refer to the resultant inflammation as "osteochondritis."

Whatever the underlying cause, some joints affected with OC eventually develop flaps of cartilage that are loosely attached to the surfaces of the joint or loose bodies of cartilage within the joint. (When these things are seen, the condition is usually called osteochondritis dissecans, or OCD; the "dissecans" refers to the flap of cartilage that dissects off the joint surface.) Cartilage flaps most often occur in the hock, stifle and shoulder joints of horses.

Yet another manifestation of OC is a collapse of the joint cartilage. In some cases, this shows up as holes in the bone underneath the cartilage (these are called cysts). Cysts under the cartilage have been reported in virtually every joint of both limbs of the horse. Another type of cartilage collapse can be seen in the hocks of young horses; this type of OC is occasionally referred to as "juvenile bone spavin."

It's not too hard to understand that abnormalities or irregularities in the joint surface or bone underneath the joint surfaces can eventually cause inflammation in the joint. If inflammation occurs, the usual treatment is removal of the abnormal cartilage flaps or elimination of the cyst (the cyst is sort of routed out using a drill) by arthroscopic surgery. Studies on horses that have had surgery for treatment of OC have shown that many horses do very well after surgery; predictably, the more cartilage that is involved, the worse the problem is and the less likely it is that surgery will have a successful outcome.

What's harder to understand is why *all* horses with OC don't develop joint problems. Chunks of cartilage in various joints are often picked up during routine prepurchase examinations in horses that have never shown (and are not currently showing) any signs of lameness. While many of these horses never seem to develop any joint problems, others may eventually need surgery. Unfortunately, there's absolutely no way to tell which horse is going to eventually develop arthritis related to a quiet OC problem, so if you are going to buy a horse with an OC problem, you have to do it with your fingers crossed.

Of course, the ideal solution to the problem of OC would be to prevent the condition in the first place. However, that will undoubtedly not be as easy as it sounds (is anything?). As a practical matter, since there appear to be some hereditary factors involved in the development of the condition, the problem may be to some extent unavoidable, particularly if you choose to breed horses that have OC. Heredity may be more than simply a passing on of a problem from parents who had the problem, however. For example, the incidence of OC appears to increase in horses that are excessively heavy for their age and bones as with halter horses. The size of the horse, rather than merely a genetic tendency to develop OC, may be an important hereditary component that leads to the development of the condition. Furthermore, unavoidable mechanical factors such as excessive exercise, abnormalities in limb conformation, large body size relative to the amount of bone or excessive weight bearing on one limb when the other one is affected with lameness also appear to be involved in the development of OC.

Nutritional factors related to OC have also been given a lot of attention. Diets that supply too many calories, those that are high in phosphorus or zinc or those that are low in copper can be associated with the occurrence of OC. Of course, some of these nutritional factors may also relate to other factors; for example, the young horse that is getting fed a lot of calories to get him to grow bigger faster is also the horse that is going to tend to be too big for his bones.

Feeding the growing horse properly is not merely a matter of starving him to prevent growth or providing lots of supplements either. Giving vitamins and minerals willy-nilly to growing horses has been shown to *cause* bone and cartilage problems in horses. If you are trying to eliminate feed-related OC problems, the best thing to do is try to come up with a balanced feed ration that's based on an analysis of the feeds available to the horse. Allowing the young horse to grow and develop at a normal rate may be ideal for the horse; unfortunately, given the realities and pressures of the show ring, this may not always be considered an option.

OC is a big problem for the horse industry. It's also an area in which there is a lot of research going on. Hopefully, the incidence of OC will be reduced as the underlying causes of the condition are more fully understood. However, given the multiplicity of causes of the condition, it's likely that OC is always going to be a potential problem in the joints of horses.

## Joint Infections

Joint infections are the most extreme type of acute inflammation that can happen in a joint. Infections are caused by bacteria that find their way into a joint; the infection is accompanied by severe inflammation that can, if treatment fails, lead to destruction of a joint and osteoarthritis.

The bacteria that infect joints cause all sorts of havoc. White blood cells from the bloodstream come racing into the joint to help fight off the infection; unfortunately, these cells release chemicals and enzymes that, while designed to destroy bacteria, have the unwanted side effect of destroying joint cartilage as well. Joint infections also affect the joint capsule and synovial membrane, causing thickening and impairing the function of these important structures.

Bacteria can find their way into joints via a number of routes. Among the most common (in order of occurrence) are:

1. After wounds that enter a joint.
2. After injections into a joint.
3. After joint surgery.
4. As a result of systemic infections in foals, where the infection enters the joint via the bloodstream (in such conditions as "navel ill").
5. Odd cases for which a cause is not apparent.

The signs of a joint infection are just like those of any case of acute arthritis, but they're usually worse. That is, infected joints tend to be extremely swollen and painful. You can usually suspect that a joint is infected from the history that precedes the problem; for example, if your horse got a shot of something into his joint a few days ago and today he can't walk, it's reasonable to suspect that there could be some sort of a problem related to the injection. If that problem is an infection, it needs to be treated right away. Treatment for joint infections is directed at cleaning out the joint, fighting the joint inflammation and killing the bacteria that cause the problem.

Cleaning out an infected joint is a matter of rinsing the joint out (lavage). Lavage is the equivalent of swishing out your mouth (see chapter 6). Some infected joints can even be managed by cutting into the joint and leaving it open; the infected fluid can drain out the open hole rather than accumulating in the joint. (Obviously, these are techniques that should be done under clean conditions, preferably in a hospital and under the direction of a veterinarian.)

Fighting inflammation in a joint involves any or all of the physical or medical therapies that were mentioned in earlier chapters. A notable exception is that corticosteroid drugs are *never* used to treat infections. Although these drugs are potent suppressors of inflammation, they also suppress the immune reaction that's needed to get rid of the infection.

Killing the bacteria involves the use of antibiotics. Most of the antibiotics that are commonly used in the horse have been evaluated in the treatment of joint infections. Joint fluid or synovial membrane can be cultured in a laboratory in an effort to isolate the bacteria that is causing the infection; if the bacteria can be isolated, antibiotics that kill that bacteria can be selected and used for treatment. Unfortunately, this is rarely as easy as it sounds; frequently bacterial cultures of joint fluid and synovial membrane fail to grow bacteria.

It's fairly well accepted that the antibiotics that are given to fight the infection in the joint should be given systemically (that is, in the vein, muscle or orally) rather than being placed directly into the joint. That's because it's been shown that putting antibiotics directly into the joint causes its own inflammation. In addition, antibiotics that are put into the joint are fairly rapidly removed from the joint, whereas antibiotics that are placed into the horse circulate in the bloodstream and help maintain a level of the drug in the joint.

A successful recovery from a joint infection hinges on early recognition of the problem and aggressive treatment. If the infection can be taken care of before secondary changes to the cartilage occur in the joint, the chances of a full recovery are good. However, if the infection is uncontrolled or secondary changes occur, osteoarthritis (or worse) may be the unfortunate result.

# EPILOGUE

IF IT HAS DONE NOTHING ELSE, HOPEFULLY THIS BOOK has taught you what a difficult problem arthritis can be to manage. Happily, many cases of acute arthritis can be managed in any number of ways to a successful outcome. The flip side of the coin is that many cases of osteoarthritis don't respond well to any treatment. At the very least, after reading this book you should understand your treatment options and approach treatment with reasonable expectations of success.

It's important to be involved in the treatment of your horse's arthritis. Aggressive management of acute arthritis will help lead to a successful outcome; careful treatment of osteoarthritis may help prolong the career of a good friend and companion. There are many ways in which you can handle the problem of arthritis; keep in mind that the most expensive treatment is not necessarily the best. Make sure that you question your veterinarian thoroughly prior to beginning any treatment and understand what it is that you are trying to do. Don't forget to ask if and how you can become involved in your horse's physical therapy if you have the time or the inclination to provide it. In that way, you'll be more likely to end up with a good result or at least understand why the result you got wasn't all that great.

# Epilogue

Given all the research that goes on in the field of arthritis, it's likely that newer and better treatments are ahead for the years to come. Unfortunately, due to the size and power of the horse, it's unlikely that joint replacement surgeries will ever be a viable treatment option (as they are in humans and dogs). However, as researchers begin to unlock the mysteries of joint cartilage and learn how to replace it or to promote its repair, the goal of returning a joint to normal, rather than just controlling the inflammation in the joint, may eventually be achieved.

Fortunately, there is excellent research that is being done to address the problems. The Equine Orthopedic Research Program at Colorado State University has focused on joint disease in the horse for the past eighteen years; a considerable amount of the information in this book comes from their research. The research program at CSU has expanded into a major interdisciplinary effort that is focusing on critical issues in equine arthritis, such as:

- Finding a way to repair joint cartilage once it is lost.
- Diagnosis of joint cartilage deterioration and injury to the bone at its earliest stages using blood tests and synovial markers.
- Defining the early events of traumatic joint injury and its detection before overt fractures occur.
- New methods of treating traumatic inflammation of the joint capsule (synovitis and capsulitis), including the use of gene therapy.

This is important work, not only for horses but for all species. For further information, contact the Equine Sciences Program at Colorado State University, Fort Collins, CO 80523-1679; by telephone at (970) 491-8542; or at their Web site at www.colostate.edu/depts/equine/. They deserve your support.

# BIBLIOGRAPHY

Balch, O., K. White and D. Butler. "Factors Involved in the Balancing of Equine Hooves." *Journal of the American Veterinary Association*, 198 no. 11 (1990): 1980–89.

Bucci, L. R. *Nutrition Applied to Rehabilitation and Sports Medicine*. Boca Raton, Fla.: CRC Press, 1995: 177–203.

"Joint Lameness." Proceedings of the 42nd Annual Convention of the American Association of Equine Practitioners, 1996.

McIlwraith, C. W. and G. Trotter. *Joint Disease in the Horse*. Philadelphia: W. B. Saunders and Co., 1996.

White, N. A. and J. N. Moore. *Current Practice of Equine Surgery*. Philadelphia: J. B. Lippincott Co., 1990.

# INDEX